PEOPLE POWER

People Power

John R. Noe

OLIVER
NELSON

A Division of Thomas Nelson Publishers
Nashville • Atlanta • Camden • New York

Published in Nashville, Tennessee, by Oliver-Nelson Books, a division of Thomas Nelson, Inc., Publishers, and distributed in Canada by Lawson Falle, Ltd., Cambridge, Ontario.

Printed in the United States of America.

The Bible version used in this publication is THE NEW KING JAMES VERSION. Copyright © 1979, 1980, 1982, Thomas Nelson, Inc., Publishers.

The quotation on page 21 is taken from IN HIS IMAGE, by Dr. Paul Brand and Philip Yancey. Copyright © 1984. Used by permission.

The quotation on page 82 is taken from MARY KAY ON PEOPLE MANAGEMENT by Mary K. Ash. Copyright © 1984. Used by permission.

The quotation on page 88 is from Charles Mergendahl's THE NEXT BEST THING, extracted in THE ENCYCLOPEDIA OF RELIGIOUS QUOTATIONS, ed. and comp. Ed S. Mead (Westwood, N.J.: Revell, 1965), p. 282.

The stories of Alfons Franzen on page 77, the six principles on page 94, and Clarence Cagle on page 112 are based on material previously published in PEAK PERFORMANCE PRINCIPLES FOR HIGH ACHIEVERS by John R. Noe. Copyright © 1984.

The sled dog story on page 92 is from an article in USAIR Magazine by Lorna Coppinger. Used by permission.

Unless specifically identified as factual, all names and events have been fictionalized for protection of privacy.

Library of Congress Cataloging-in-Publication Data

Noe, John R., 1945–
  People power.

  1. Interpersonal relations. 2. Success. I. Title.
HM132.N64   1986   158'.2   86-18027
ISBN 0-8407-9063-5

D E D I C A T I O N

With love to my children,
Elise and Ken, whose zest
for life provides me with
some of my best material.

C O N T E N T S

THANK YOU ix
PREFACE xi
INTRODUCTION 13

SECTION ONE
Why Dynamic Responsiveness
Can Make a Difference

1 Why Even the Lone Ranger Had a Sidekick 19
2 Why Connecting with People Leads
   to High Achievement 28
3 Why a Systems Approach Works with People 48
4 Why the Dynamic Responsiveness System
   Gets Results 64
5 Why You Should Be a Responsive Person
   in an Unresponsive World 90

SECTION TWO
How to Master the Skills
of Dynamic Responsiveness

6 How to Listen Responsively 105
7 How to Communicate Responsively 122

8 How to Set Goals for High Achievement 143
9 How to Plan for Responsive Action 155
10 How to Choose and Channel People
   for High Achievement 167
11 How to Equip People for High Achievement 180
12 How to Hold Responsive Meetings 196
13 How to Be a Tiger, Not a Pussycat 210

T H A N K Y O U

My gratitude goes to the people and corporations who have engaged me and our firm to motivate, train, educate, or manage their employees. They have all helped greatly in the growth of our corporation and the enhancement of my work.

Without a doubt, the hardest part of writing a book like *People Power* is not the effort of writing it, but the challenge of living it daily. I'm indebted to those who know me well, for their practical advice and persistent stimulation—to all my colleagues in Industrial Housekeeping Management Systems; to Jerry VanGombos, executive, whose people power far exceeds mine; to Victor Oliver, my publisher who believed in me; to Nido Qubein, my friend whose insights and support I cherish; but most of all, to my wife, Cindy, for the hours she has invested listening to me, counseling me, and loving me in the pursuit of high achievement.

To all these loving and responsive people, I give one big Thank You!

Most of us would be much more responsive to those we love and those we work with if it were not for one great fear: We are afraid of what people will do to us. Really.

You've probably known for a long time that the best way to get people to respond to you is for you to respond to them—to their needs, desires, and concerns. Yet, like most of us, you hold back because you fear others will walk all over you or, worse, reject you outright.

Well, I've got some great news for you! Responsive people are not pussycats, they're tigers! They reach out and grab life by the throat, they walk right up to their enemies and claim them as friends, and they reap the benefits of giving freely of themselves.

Responsive people know the secrets of *People Power*. In these pages, I'll guide you step by step through the Dynamic Responsiveness System, which has been tested and proven in the "laboratory of life" for high achievement in all relationships—whether in your family and social life or in your work environment. What I propose here is based on one simple premise: What has worked for me will also work for you. I'll show you why, and I'll tell you how.

People Power is about the amazing results that occur when you learn to relate to and work successfully with other people. It is about you and what you can do to shape (rather than be shaped by) the people and events in your environment.

Absent are all the psychological findings, management theories, and business administration jargon that usually sound good on paper but have little to do with the pragmatics of relating positively to people. Each chapter will give you something to use immediately, in real life.

I believe *People Power* is a book born for the late eighties and the early nineties because it is attuned to the individualized style of intelligent people who want to be stimulated but still think for themselves. Thus, it draws from ageless truths and builds bridges for personal insights and applications.

People Power is designed as a sequel to *Peak Performance Principles for High Achievers*. Although it can be read alone, it picks up where the first work leaves off (with high achievement for the individual) and launches into the broader world of human relationships.

People Power. It is an adventure in human relations.

INTRODUCTION

Ours is a high-tech world in which machines, electronic devices, and gadgets are getting more and more attention. We are reminded of our world's technological bent every time we dial a nonworking number and hear a singsong voice say, "The number you have reached has been changed. The new number is. . . ." We worry that our children will not do well in school if they do not have access to a computer or that our businesses will lag behind if they are not properly equipped for this computer age. Holographic scanners reading prices at the checkout counter and automatic bank tellers dispensing money are more evidence of the rapid rise of high technology.

To protest against technology would be to protest the dawn. Economics and cultural realities make its progress certain, even desirable. I'm all for advancements in medicine, in business, and in the quality of life in general. My purpose for writing this book is not to protest the increasing significance of gadgetry in our lives. My purpose is to provide focus for keeping our priorities straight.

Let's face it. It may be generally conceded that the most vital factor in the success of any venture is people, but for all the lip service given to it, people power is still the least understood element of most families and of most business endeavors. Let's face it. It matters little how much we improve the quality of life unless we also make life worth living. Gadgets can never do that. Our success, happiness, and reason for living are more dependent than ever on the human factor. We need human response. We need other people.

Whether we manage an organization, work for a corporation, buy or sell, fellowship in a church, or live with people we love, our most pressing need (next to maintaining our relationship with God) is the need to know how to get the most from our human relationships. We need people power.

It's not unusual for us to flip on the radio first thing in the morning to hear newscasters announcing that a revolution has occurred in some third world country while we slept. Revolutions seem to happen very quickly, and we hear about them almost instantly. But revolutions almost never happen that quickly. The fires of revolution begin as tiny sparks in the hearts of a few people, smoulder for months (sometimes decades), then suddenly burst into open flame. The longer revolutions smoulder before erupting, the more successful they tend to be.

All of which leads me to ask, are we sleeping through the *electronic* revolution? Are we like Washington Irving's mythical character who slept for twenty years? After his long sleep, Rip Van Winkle awoke oblivious to the fact that the American colonists had overthrown the British kingdom. And he found himself in a peck of trouble when he started greeting old friends with "God save the King!"

Yet revolutions are like that. They creep up on us. They don't seem to be revolutionary at all. It's easy to ignore prophetic voices that warn something big is going on. Did we really hear Marshall McLuhan, in the sixties, when he told us that the electronic media were reshaping our world into a "global village," and that our values, our economies, and our whole world were being restructured by their "message"? And did we listen to Alvin Toffler, in the seventies, when he warned that "change is avalanching upon our heads and most people are grotesquely unprepared to cope with it"? Or did we take seriously enough his signals, in the early eighties, that we were moving rapidly toward the "electronic cottage," where the home again would become the work center of our society?

Sure, we notice the high-tech takeover when we call to get a service and a machine answers. We notice it when we receive a computerized revolving charge statement showing a million dollars due. But do we notice television's computer-generated graphics that were technically impossible in the seventies? Do we notice the page-one story in the *Wall Street Journal* about psychologists and hypnotists who are selling computer software to reprogram minds through subliminal messages?

We need only compare the employment ads of today with those of twenty years ago to discover just how business has changed its requirements for hiring people. The emphasis used to be on "good work records" and "honesty" and "ambition." Now the ads focus more and more on technical skills, experience with certain types of equipment, and higher levels of educational attainment. The shift from "what kind of person you are" to "what you can do" is subtle, but the implications are clear. The business climate in which people are paramount is changing to a climate in which the new technology is paramount.

When recruiting managers and executives, more and more businesses tend to ask, "What was your bottom-line record last year?" rather than, "Can you work effectively with people?" These businesses reason that when the new person begins to falter in performance, he or she can be replaced. Such a short-term view will lead to long-term trouble.

Dehumanized attitudes and practices are the natural result when business and society shift emphasis from people power to high-tech capabilities. We call that process *dehumanizing* because it makes us less than human.

My growing awareness of this dehumanizing trend in our world spurred me to write this book. Certainly the more we drift toward dehumanization, the less we treat other people as fully human creatures of God.

- *What if* the key to all real success, happiness, and health is in learning how to work effectively with other people?
- *What if* the greatest discoveries ahead lie in unlocking our human potential among one another?
- *What if* the Bible's claim that we are all made in the image of God means we have yet to discover the tremendous potential we have as individuals and as groups of people?
- *What if* Jesus of Nazareth is actually a prototype of the kind of person God has in mind for all of us to become?
- *What if* our human destinies are so bound up with the people around us that we can only truly be ourselves when we are in harmony with those people?

I believe all of those *what if's* are true. And the possibilities for reversing the dehumanizing process—a shift to rehumanization through people power—are tremendously exciting!

SECTION
ONE

Why Dynamic
Responsiveness Can
Make a Difference

Before we can discuss developing the "how" skills that will help us become dynamic, responsive people, we need to come to an understanding of "why" Dynamic Responsiveness can make a difference in an increasingly unresponsive world.

The coupling of the why's with the how's (or the educational with the technical) in the two sections of this book gives *People Power* meaning and purpose and enhances the long-term benefit for the reader.

The Dynamic Responsiveness System is based on sound principles that can help you achieve worthy goals in your family, business, and organizations. But before you can begin to practice the Dynamic Responsiveness System, you must have confidence in yourself and your abilities. Chapter One clarifies why you need to cooperate in our highly connected world. Next, Chapter Two explains why connecting with people leads to high achievement. Then, Chapter Three illustrates why a systems approach works with people, and Chapter Four explores why the Dynamic Responsiveness System gets results. Finally, in this section, Chapter Five takes a look at why you should be a responsive person in an unresponsive world.

Let's get started on our adventure. The sooner you learn why living responsively can make a difference, the sooner you can apply Dynamic Responsiveness to your life.

ONE

Why Even the Lone Ranger Had a Sidekick

MYTH: High-tech gadgets will do away with your job and do you in. What you can do no longer matters. People don't count for much any more.

FACT: *You* can make good things happen in your life and in the lives of others through *people power*.

Many of us are feeling more and more like passive spectators in this age of high-tech convenience. The more technology does for or to us, the less confident we feel about our abilities to make a difference. Computers. Word processors. Robotics. Microwave ovens. Direct dialing. Conference calls. Digital instrument panels. Head phones. Video games. Automatic bank tellers. Direct deposit. Holographic pricing scanners. Remote-control television. Instant replays. Cable TV. Satellite relay systems.

The technological advances we now enjoy—advances that could be used to bring people closer together—are resulting in increased isolation of the individual. It's too easy to enjoy the world vicariously, to sit back and watch it on TV, to read about it in the newspaper, to hear about it on the radio. That's not the way our lives have to be. Our lives can be exciting adventures with other people.

It is time we realize our potential, become active participants instead of passive spectators in life, and live more harmoniously by learning to relate and work with other people.

Let's call it *synergism*, defined as "cooperative action of discrete agencies such that the total effect is greater than the sum of the effects taken independently." In plain language it means that we can get a whole lot more done when we work together.

Look back to July 20, 1969, to get an idea of what human beings can accomplish when they work together. "That's one small step for man; one giant leap for mankind," came Neil Armstrong's famous speech of less than a complete sentence. What made it so momentous was that it was spoken from the surface of the moon.

Not one of those three astronauts (Neil Armstrong, Edwin E. Aldrin, or Michael Collins) could have gone to the moon alone. In fact, the three of them working furiously together could not have accomplished so great a feat. Their triumph was the product of the direct work of thousands of people, and the indirect participation of millions.

Yet, as impressive as that achievement was, reaching the moon is only a small example of what human beings can accomplish when we work together.

The human body illustrates perfectly the tremendous power of synergism. It is made up of trillions of cells so tiny we cannot see them with the naked eye. Yet each microscopic cell performs a function that is essential for the whole body to function in the fantastic way it does.

In my professional life, I spend most of my time directing a corporation that trains and supervises industrial housekeeping operations in several of America's largest manufacturing facilities. The task of the people we work with is to make sure huge plants are kept clean and ready for action. Therefore, I was fascinated by Dr. Paul Brand's explanation of how the human body is constantly cleansing itself with its blood and cleansing organs. In his excellent book *In His Image*, the world-renowned surgeon says:

The body performs its janitorial duties with such impressive speed and efficiency that I cannot resist at least a summary of them. . . . No cell lies more than a hair's breadth from a blood capillary, lest poisonous by-products pile up and cause . . . ill effects. . . . Through a basic chemical process of gas diffusion and transfer, individual red blood cells drifting along inside narrow capillaries simultaneously release their cargoes of fresh oxygen and absorb waste products (carbon dioxide, urea, and uric acid, etc.) from these cells. The red cells then deliver the hazardous waste chemicals to the organs that can dump them outside the body.

In the lungs, carbon dioxide collects in small pockets to be exhaled with every breath. . . . Complex chemical wastes are left to a more discriminating organ, the kidney. . . . After the kidney has removed the red cell's entire payload to extract some thirty chemicals, its enzymes promptly reinsert 99 percent of the volume into the bloodstream. The 1 percent remaining, mostly urea, is hustled away to the bladder to await expulsion. . . .

Other organs enter the scavenging process also. A durable red cell can only sustain the rough sequence of freight-loading and unloading for a half million circuits or so until, battered and leaky as a worn-out river barge, it nudges its way to the liver and spleen for one last unloading. This time, the red cell itself is picked clean, broken down into amino acids and bile pigments for recycling. . . . A new cycle of fueling and cleansing begins.

That's just one example of how the various cells and organs of the human body work together in a synergy so magnificent and effective that we only notice its operation when something goes wrong.

No wonder Sophocles, writing thousands of years before modern medical science discovered how complex the human body really is, said, "Numberless are the world's wonders, but none—none more wondrous than the body of man."

ANATOMY OF A HUMAN SYNERGISM

What if we could come anywhere close to the kind of powerful synergy God has built into our individual bodies in our human relationships? Can you imagine what a joy life would be, how much more each of us could accomplish individually, and how much we could get done collectively?

Let's look briefly at how different parts of the human body work together under strenuous use, and what that suggests about our relating to different people. It will give us an overview of what we'll spend the remainder of the book exploring together.

Similarity 1: Interrelation

When I climbed to the top of "the world's most classic mountain," the Matterhorn in Switzerland, my whole body was involved. It would be foolish to say my arms did all of the work, or my legs carried me to the peak, or my brain gave me the power to do it. I can't tell you how delighted I was that John Noe—the whole person—made it successfully to the crest of that awesome tiger of the Alps and back down again.

My feet cautiously searched for solid foundations to anchor my whole body; my legs provided leverage to lift my weight higher and higher; my arms and hands searched for strongholds to grasp; my lungs struggled in the thin air to keep an adequate supply of oxygen for my whole body; my heart worked overtime to keep me from freezing and to give me the energy to keep climbing.

During the two years of training for that climb, I ran along the back roads of Indiana. I kept looking down at my feet and saying, "One day these feet are going to stand on top of the Matterhorn!" But it would have been a meaningless accomplishment if my feet had been the only part of me to make it. Had my feet been cut off in a rock slide, my guide Alfons Franzen could have strapped them onto his back and carried them all the way to the top. The picture I have in our family scrapbook, the one that shows my feet on top of the Matterhorn, has meaning only because my feet were attached to me.

> None of us can truly say,
> "I am,"
> until he or she can truly say,
> "We are."

Just as God designed the human body to be interrelated, God designed human beings to be interrelated. None of us can truly say, "I am," until he or she can truly say, "*We* are!"

"No man is an island, entire of itself," said John Donne in *Devotions upon Emergent Occasions.* "Any man's death diminishes me, because I am involved in mankind; and therefore never send to know for whom the bell tolls; it tolls for thee," he concluded.

The sooner we more fully come to grips with our interrelatedness with other human beings, the happier, more productive, and respected we can be.

Similarity 2: Interdependence

How interdependent are our body parts? Think about a severely sprained ankle. We usually become aware of this injury through pain, because a sprained ankle can make the whole body ache and even feel nauseated. But a whole lot more is involved than pain, and what happens is so automatic that we are not conscious that it's going on.

At the moment of the injury, nerves send a distress signal to the brain at lightning speed. Instantly, the whole body goes into action to pick up the slack from the injured member. The other leg flexes to take over the strain; the arms shoot outward to break the fall; the whole body reflexes to shift the weight to the uninjured leg. The whole body springs to the aid of the injured member in ways we don't understand. Glands secrete adrenaline to give a burst of added strength. The heart beats faster to provide more oxygen to meet the increased demand. And if the pain is severe enough, we may lapse into unconsciousness to make it bearable. The pain functions to alert the other members of the body to take up the slack so that the hurt ankle is enabled to heal.

There's no fixing of blame, only efforts to fix the problem. There's no good leg saying to an injured leg, "You dummy! Look what you've done!" You won't find the hands saying, "I keep telling you feet to look where you're going!"

Unfortunately, few human relationships ever come close to recognizing that kind of interdependence. Family relationships are usually the only ones that approach it, but too often families recognize how much they need a member only after that member is gone.

People may threaten our security, hurt us severely, frustrate us, and make us angry enough to blow a fuse. But nothing we can do about their actions, nor any emotion we may feel, can change the fact that we need other people.

When a family member breaks an arm, the rest of the family usually works together to do that person's chores and help the individual get through the daily routine. Many times when a baby is born into a family, relatives and friends cooperate to assist the new parents—from bringing food to offering reliable baby-sitting services.

In the business world, when one employee goes on vacation, others adjust their schedules so that the work will be done. I've read in the newspaper of more than one businessman who lost his store and his goods to a natural disaster such as a fire, and other local business people made available their time and services until the individual could get back on his feet again.

Too many of us are reluctant to depend on others for help in doing our jobs. A friend told me of his own experience that clearly illustrates this point. He would take home stacks of paperwork that just had to be done—by him. As a result, he rarely spent time after dinner with his wife and nine-year-old daughter. One night he heard his daughter say, "Mommy, why does Daddy bring home his briefcase each night?" Trying to be positive about the situation, her mother replied, "Your father has an important position and a lot of responsibility at work. He's in charge of many people, and he just doesn't have enough time to get everything done at the office." "Well," the youngster replied, "why don't they put Daddy in a slower group?" After that, my friend said he made a point of delegating more work to the qualified people in his office, and he concentrated on things that required his special expertise. He realized that he had unnecessarily assumed too great a work load, and he was able to adapt a more normal work schedule when he was willing to rely and depend upon others.

Similarity 3: Interaction

The human body has tremendous power because of the way its various members interact with each other. For example, humans are the only creatures in the animal kingdom who have opposing thumbs. The interaction between the thumb and four fingers is such a common thing that few of us ever think about it. Yet that simple capability enables us to use our hands in ways that are far superior to the lower animals.

People who understand the simple concept of interaction in human relationships can accomplish almost superhuman feats. You'll find them conducting symphonies, constructing huge skyscrapers and bridges, saving lives, and acting in many other ways we call heroic.

> People who understand the simple concept
> of interaction in human relationships
> can accomplish almost superhuman feats.

Our forebears recognized the value of interaction, even though some of the ways they utilized it may not seem heroic in the strictest sense of the word. Gathering together to raise a home or a barn was a significant effort that oftentimes guaranteed the survival of a family or a family's livelihood, such as animals or a harvest. Building up communities that have become today's towns and cities required interaction on all levels; workers, merchants, bankers, industrialists, and so on played various roles in these endeavors.

Unlike animals who are capable only of passing on the same information from generation to generation (today's baby beavers learn the exact dam-building skills their great-great-grandparents learned), human beings have a tremendous capacity to collect and store information, connect it with information stored previously, draw conclusions, and then devise new, improved ways of doing things. In other words, we can learn from our ancestors, accept advanced teaching from our contemporaries, and pass it on to the next generation. What a glorious God-given capacity!

TYING IT ALL TOGETHER

The further we go technologically, the more we need to understand and be able to work with other people. It is crucial for us to recognize, make allowances for, and capitalize upon our interrelationship, our interdependence, and our interaction with other people.

Even the fictional Lone Ranger felt the need for a sidekick, Tonto. In today's highly connected world, there simply are no Lone Rangers. Our lives are a constant process of negotiating with other human beings. Each of us brings our own set of needs, desires, and struggles to life's bargaining table. Likewise, each of us brings along our talents, resources, and caring concern. Life's high achievers are those who best understand and most skillfully utilize the process. They're the ones who know how to find fulfillment, happiness, and achievement through working with other people.

CHAPTER
TWO

Why Connecting with People Leads to High Achievement

One of the most exciting things I ever discovered about myself was that I could dangle on the end of a rope—with the nearest land beneath me more than a mile away—and still be able to function. When I discovered I could lay it all on the line and trust my life to the person on the other end of the rope (a person I'd known only a few days), nothing could hold me back from climbing some of the highest and most treacherous mountains in the world.

Connecting with other people is risky business, but it's the only way we can ever hope to become high achievers. It's a little like driving an automobile. There is always the risk of being knocked off the road by a drunk or careless driver or being injured from a faulty mechanism, but taking chances is the only way we can get anywhere. The truth is that high achievers are usually very conservative in games of chance but very daring in arenas that require skill. So we work out a system that enables us to reduce our risks and to get where we want to go.

In this chapter we'll talk about (1) problems with theories; (2) fixing the problem rather than fixing the blame; (3) the differences between people and machines; and (4) why we need a system.

PROBLEMS WITH THEORIES

Working with people is too vital to leave to the empty theories that have become popular in recent decades. By empty theories, I mean ones that have letters of the alphabet or people's names attached to them. After all, where do we go after Maslow? What's next after Theory X? What'll we try after Theory Y? Oh, whee . . . now it's Theory Z?

One of the byproducts of our technological orientation is that we have come to rely almost fanatically upon so-called specialists, such as social workers, psychotherapists, and encounter group leaders. We've got industrial psychologists, management scientists, and a host of other specialists bombarding us with confusing, and often conflicting theories about how to work with people. According to one writer, "There are as many techniques, methods and theories around as there are researchers and therapists" in the field of psychology.

Computers have made it easier for psychologists to test their theories of motivation for human behavior. We've gone crazy over polls and surveys that are supposed to predict what people will do in any given situation. Giant data banks contain millions of bytes of information about all of us. This information enables specialists in human behavior to study, analyze, and project our attitudes, actions, and responses in every conceivable way.

We use elaborate and sophisticated equipment to stage conference calls and motivational meetings and to communicate with increasing numbers of people each day. Closed circuit television networks are replacing bulletin boards; computer modems are transferring huge volumes of data; and memos are being transmitted almost instantly from coast to coast. Our technology is making us the most connected society in history.

Yet for all our connectedness technologically, we are the

most *dis*connected people of any generation. The more we put people in touch with one another technologically, the less we connect with one another mentally, emotionally, and spiritually. We're finding it easier to "reach out" than to "touch someone."

Our alienation shows up in significant ways.

1. *The family.* Divorces have increased each year since World War II. More than 40 percent of all school-age children do not live with both their natural parents. Each year more than a million teenagers run away from home.
2. *Personal life.* Telephone counseling services consistently report that more than 90 percent of the people who call them each year call because they are lonely—they simply want to hear a friendly voice. This sense of aloneness, isolation, and disconnectedness results in rampant alcoholism and drug addiction, widespread feelings of inferiority, and what one leading psychiatrist called "the epidemic of depression."
3. *The workplace.* Bosses misunderstand the needs, goals, and concerns of workers. Workers find themselves in conflict with their supervisors and coworkers. Orders are not carried out, costly mistakes are made, productivity suffers, and customers often are made to feel unwanted.

Yet for all our connectedness
technologically, we are the most
*dis*connected people
of any generation.

How can these things be? How can it be that we have so many specialists to explain human behavior and tell us how to get people to do what we want them to do, and yet we fail so often in our most significant relationships? How can we be so progressive in working with machines, yet so backward in relating to people?

Problem 1: Theories Must Be Tested

The basic problem with theories is that they are just that—theories. The so-called science of human behavior is not a science at all; it is an art. An art deals with creative arrangements producing form or beauty, and the elements that make our art what it is are very difficult to test objectively. A science, on the other hand, deals with established knowledge, and principles, elements that can be more readily tested. In a science, a theory is only a point for beginning, a hypothesis to be proved or disproved in a laboratory or in real life. However elaborate their premises, however scientific their data, theories of human behavior must be tested.

Perhaps that's why the major theories of human behavior change every few decades. Far too many frustrated family members and corporate executives run from seminar to seminar, conference to conference, this group to that group searching for the newest "pop" psychology only to come away with a few more shallow ideas. Ever since the industrial revolution a hundred and fifty years ago in America, management people have been lining up behind one theory after another to try to increase productivity in the workplace.

Prior to the industrial revolution, most workers were their own managers. They were either farmers or craftsmen who saw their work through from beginning to end. As productivity and profits became increasingly important, two distinct classes began to emerge—workers and managers. Large and small corporations started giving most of their attention to how to make the worker become a more useful part of the overall production machine. That was the beginning of human resource management.

During the 1880s, Frederick Taylor advanced his theory of *Scientific Management,* which held that timing workers' movements and setting minimum production standards would increase productivity. That theory is still widely used today in some circles. Taylor's principles of work led directly to the reshaping of human beings in the machine image. These "machine" beings are quite different from the men and women who have been carefully sculpted in God's own image.

Scientific Management was virtually unopposed until the early 1900s when researchers at the Hawthorne Works of the Western Electric plant in Illinois developed the *Hawthorne Studies.* They had stumbled onto the observation that the more attention workers perceived they were receiving from management, the more productive they tended to be. The Hawthorne Studies gave rise to the *Human Relations* school of thought in managing people.

Managers who utilized the Human Relations concept treated workers as complex human beings with feelings, motives, and desires, not just as individuals capable of performing certain tasks. Because social and psychological factors were thought to have the greatest influence on the willingness to work, managers offered friendly supervision based on trust and confidence in workers. It was believed that people would respond to these efforts by being happier and more satisfied on the job and thus more productive.

In the 1930s and 1940s, Abraham Maslow, a psychologist, developed what he called the *Theory of Human Motivation.* According to Maslow, people sought to satisfy their needs in a hierarchy. He held that people start with the basic needs of hunger, thirst, shelter, and sex. Once those needs are met, people then move to satisfy their needs for safety (security), love, and self-esteem. Armed with that theory, managers began to systematically attempt to provide conditions that would allow people to satisfy some of those needs in the workplace.

In 1959, researcher Frederick Herzberg advanced the theory that eliminating all dissatisfaction from the work environment would not necessarily make people more satisfied, only less dissatisfied. Herzberg identified hygiene factors—fringe benefits, job security, working conditions, wages, and fair treatment on the job—that can lessen job dissatisfaction.

Yet satisfactory hygiene factors cannot motivate workers, and unsatisfactory ones can even demotivate them. To actually motivate workers to want to do better, Herzberg said that management should offer motivators such as opportunities for personal growth, recognition, advancement, and achievement; providing interesting work that carries some responsibility with it should also have positive effects in the workplace.

With a massive invasion of imports from Japan during the 1960s and 1970s, managers began asking what the Japanese were doing that was right, and they discovered *Quality of Work Life* (QWL). QWL began to catch on in America, and its offspring, the *quality circle,* has gained widespread acceptance. Basically, the quality circle is a meeting of workers (not just foremen or managers) engaged directly in various levels of the production process. They discuss ways of putting quality control into practice, attempting to improve the product quality as well as lower costs and increase volume. Quality circles are found not only in industries producing goods but also in some service industries such as banking. A greater commitment to automation and an increased reliance on computers have occurred along with the popularity of the quality circle.

There is little question that all these theories have played a role in building some of American industry to a place of world leadership. Yet the productivity of individual workers continues to be a major cause for concern among managers and business leaders.

What good is technology if we are faced with a disenchanted work force? What good is interactive television if we cannot interact with those who live in our own homes? What good does it do to reach out halfway around the world if we can't touch someone we really care about?

> What good does it do to
> reach out halfway around the world
> if we can't touch someone
> we really care about?

Problem 2: Theories Fail to Predict Human Behavior

"If We Can Send a Man to the Moon . . . ?" If we can do that, why can't we do this? It's a question that has been asked thousands of times, in thousands of ways, about thousands of human dilemmas—yet it always expresses the same kind of frustration. Theories can enable us to accomplish great things technologically, but they break down when we try to apply them to human relationships.

If we can send a man to the moon, why can't we

. . . heal the brokenness in marriages?

. . . enable fathers and sons, mothers and daughters to talk to and love each other?

. . . motivate workers to give their best in their jobs?

. . . end the adversarial climate in American industry?

. . . gain cooperation from people we work with every day?

. . . negotiate satisfactory agreements among people with whom we desire to do business?

If those questions are compelling now, they will become even more so in the years ahead. In fact, it seems the more we have to do with high-tech machines, the less able we are to communicate with people.

Scientific theories readily fit machines. If you learn a few laws of mathematics, for example, you can easily master the computer.

In Professor Toffler's electronic cottage, children who grow up in a high-tech environment are able to master the most sophisticated equipment with ease. We already see symptoms of it, and we see its theme being used in more and more commercials. Dad buys a home computer, and while he sits down to read the instructions to see how to hook the thing up and get it working, Junior plugs it in and starts running programs. That same kid, however, may be having difficulty with basic human communications. Or with getting along with other children. Or with expressing his deepest feelings.

I'm sure you've seen people in the workplace who can make the most complicated equipment sing but can't harmonize with anyone in their department. Actually, that might describe your own experience. If people will just stay out of your way, you can get all kinds of work done. But if you try to work with other people, or try to get others to work together, everything seems to bog down.

I'm a little mystified by people who say they want to be with their friends and then choose a disco for their place to get together. With loud music vibrating, strobe lights pulsating, and some guy blasting away, people try to enjoy each other. When the music stops, any hint of quiet is destroyed by trivial patter reverberating through a deafening public address system. Sound familiar? And we wonder why we feel lonely so much of the time!

FIXING THE PROBLEM RATHER THAN FIXING THE BLAME

High technology can be pretty heady stuff. The idea is appealing that a personal computer can enable us to budget so well there's money left over to buy special luxuries. In actual practice, most people have difficulty budgeting the payments for the computer.

Managers are often lured by the common misconception that they can bring a piece of automated equipment through the front door and kick a dozen people out the back door. Experience has shown that automation almost never works that way. More often than not, effectiveness depends directly upon the degree to which people want to make automation work. The goal of business is to provide a product or service and to make a profit. However sophisticated the equipment, that goal is reached or missed as a result of how well the people who operate it work togther.

Highly motivated, highly trained people who work well together can usually get the job done even with antiquated equipment. And angry, depressed, and disenchanted people can sabotage even the best that technology can provide.

Not long ago a motivational speaker gave a rousing talk on the new spirit of the Western world. He said, "For decades, our productivity levels have been dropping. But there is a new spirit, a new determination to meet the challenge that lies ahead of us. There is a light at the end of the tunnel, and it's getting brighter. It's coming closer and closer." At this point a cynical voice from the rear of the

> Angry, depressed, and disenchanted
> people can sabotage even the best
> that technology can offer.

room interrupted him: "Yeah, it's a Japanese freight train coming straight at us!"

A GM executive, after touring our supervisory training center, explained part of the reason for the Japanese's continuing success story. He told me that we've been trying to catch up with them by investing in hardware while they've been investing in software—people. We have a lot of the same, sometimes even superior, equipment, but the Japanese figure out how to make it work better. Training is ongoing and up-to-date. Workers on all levels and of all ages are encouraged to contribute suggestions for improving their product or their service, and Japanese managers actually listen to each one. Thus, employees gain a strong sense of participation. Japanese workers are also motivated to work together because they consider their firm's success or failure to be a direct result of their group effort, and they certainly want to be part of a successful venture.

Many people feel threatened by the electronic revolution and the increased use of automation. Not everyone is like the secretary in a large office who expressed a solid opinion of her value to the company, "It would take one heckuva machine to replace me!" But there is a lot more to it than the concern about being replaced. It has to do with gaining and maintaining recognition for a job well done, with having a sense of involvement in what's happening on the job, with being able to do exciting (or at least interesting) work.

I heard recently about a staff meeting in which a chief executive officer blustered for over an hour about how work was bogging down in his high-tech office.

"We've invested a fortune to update this office!" he shouted. "And we did everything we could to make it as easy as possible for people to work. We isolated work stations so people wouldn't be bothered by interruptions. We had the whole thing color-coordinated to make it pleasant. We even piped in music! Yet we're getting less done, and making more mistakes than ever. What's wrong? I want some answers!"

"I'll tell you what's wrong!" he continued without waiting for a response. "You people are letting everybody walk all over you. If some big changes aren't made soon, heads are going to roll!"

Later, over lunch that Monday, the manager whose department had been criticized by the CEO shared with a colleague some disturbing feelings and events. The story unfolded something like this. He'd been saddled with the task of making it all work, despite his protests that he didn't feel qualified and didn't want the job. His frustrations at work caused him to become more and more depressed, and when his shaky marriage finally fell apart, he hit bottom. "I've spent the whole weekend in a motel room," he told the friend, "wondering if I should blow my brains out."

Had the CEO approached the whole problem in a different manner, the department head might have felt free to meet with the CEO privately and discuss what was going wrong and why. Who would want to open a discussion with someone who threatened to set heads rolling? Fixing the blame is hardly a positive way to get workers to cooperate. Time spent in figuring out who to blame could be much better spent evaluating the problem and trying to fix it.

DIFFERENCES BETWEEN PEOPLE
AND MACHINES

High-tech machines have been designed to imitate and enhance the tremendous capabilities of human beings. We've got simulated human voices, artificial human hearts, dreams of humanoid robots.

But machines cannot be people. Machines operate on predictable scientific principles, but people act in ways of their own choosing.

Difference 1: People Are Made in the Image
of God

First, humans are made in the image of God; machines are not. That carries with it some factors that scientific theories cannot regulate.

People have capacities and abilities that machines do not have. People can love, can laugh and cry, can feel pain and mental anguish, can create, can reason and think, and can do many things engineers can only wistfully imagine their machines doing.

The drives and motivations that shape our lives and control our actions simply don't exist in machines. As long as we must count upon human beings to make decisions, generate ideas, and deal with other people, we must remain concerned primarily with people. After all, people conceive the activities that determine the profit or loss, the success or failure, and the happiness or misery of all our ventures and relationships.

People have a spiritual dimension that machines do not have. There is something in humanity that reaches out beyond itself. As a Christian, I choose to call that something *soul* and *spirit*.

Mr. Spock, of *Star Trek* fame, is one of the most appealing characters from the futuristic world of science fiction. He is portrayed as half-human/half-Vulcan. Masses of people admire his machinelike Vulcan side that can process massive amounts of data, make superhuman analyses, and always operate logically. Many of us are intrigued by the notion of not being bound by emotions.

Yet most critics agree that what makes Mr. Spock so appealing to the masses is the occasional emergence of his human side with its caring concern, its warmth, and its morality. Often a whole television show would be built around the moment when Spock's human half would overcome his Vulcan half. When, in *Star Trek II*, the script called for Spock to die, it was for his humanity that millions of fans mourned.

Mr. Spock is fictional. But the reactions of millions of people to his adventures say clearly that most of us believe humans are different from machines, or dogs, or even robots. Something within all of us cries out for a life in the spirit dimension—a dimension that impacts strongly on everything we do in the visible world.

People have value simply because we exist. High-tech machines have value to us because of what they can do for us. When they are no longer useful to us, we discard them and replace them with more functional machines.

A great difficulty we face as a society is that many of us ignore the intrinsic value of people. People matter because people are. When love is reduced to one-night stands or live-in arrangements or what's-in-it-for-me attitudes, or when a prospective customer is nothing more than components of an integrated system, we can only expect to be disappointed with our human relationships.

If we want to connect with others, we must understand that all of us have value simply because we exist.

Difference 2: People Are Unique Beings

Second, each person is a unique being; a machine is not. When it comes to people, we can't put an individual in a line and compare that person with others because there is no line and there are no like individuals.

Scientists love the predictability and constancy of electronics and machines. The mass production system has been built around the idea of making products as nearly alike as possible. Machines can be classified, their capacities measured, and their movements programmed.

People are not so predictable. Notice what happens to an easily accessible thermostat in an office during a typical day. Some like it toasty warm, others like it rather cool, and still others like it somewhere in-between. To add to the profusion of differences, each individual likes different temperatures at different times of the day on different days.

We simply cannot lump all people together in neat little categories and predict their reactions. Certainly, we can't spend the rest of our lives trying to please everybody, but our effectiveness in working with people will depend largely upon the degree to which we recognize that each person is an individual with unique needs, concerns, and desires.

Difference 3: People Have Limitations

Third, people have limitations that machines don't have. We get tired, we have moods, we are motivated by fears and desires, we have self-images that shape everything we do. A hospital administrator once said that a hospital would run efficiently if it weren't for the patients, doctors, and nurses.

Airlines can predict with a high degree of accuracy how fast their aircraft will fly, how far they can fly on a load of fuel, and how far they must fly to reach their destination. Yet those of us who fly a lot know that our flights often will be delayed.

Since it costs a great deal of money for them to be delayed, most airlines have spent a lot of money trying to determine why they are so often running behind schedule. More often than not, delays can be traced to people.

According to theory, X number of people, given Y pieces of equipment, ought to be able to maintain Z schedules of flights. There's only one thing wrong with the theory—it doesn't work much of the time!

The problem is usually with the X number of people. People have limitations that make them unpredictable, and their limitations vary widely. However, if you removed people from the equation, aircraft would never get off the ground. It is people who make it all possible in the first place.

We can illustrate the point with a simple story. A busy executive climbed aboard a sleek new airliner one day, buckled his seat belt, and settled down for a routine flight. Twenty minutes later, a voice came over the intercom: "Good morning! Welcome to flight number 123 to Los Angeles. This plane has neither pilot nor copilot. It is being flown by the latest in electronic devices. You need not be alarmed, however, for these devices are foolproof . . . foolproof . . . foolproof. . . ."

For all its limitations, give me people power anytime!

Difference 4: People Have Personalities

Fourth, human beings have personalities; machines do not. The idea of giving names to machines (as if machines had personalities) goes back many centuries—perhaps to the practice of naming a ship after a beloved woman. Perhaps we name these inanimate objects because we gain some feeling of control over them or because we can project feelings onto them without receiving a contradictory response. By naming them, we acknowledge a kind of relationship with them, but, somehow, it's just not the same as having a relationship with another human being.

The fact is we all need person to person relationships—in our families, our schools, our community, our churches, our workplace. We need person to person relationships in every area of our lives.

It is precisely because of this need for the personal touch that human institutions can exist at all. We cannot have personal relationships with a personal computer, or a personal stereo, or a user-friendly machine. We can have personal relationships only with other people. Personal relationships make all human endeavors possible.

> People want to be treated as individuals
> with unique needs, desires, problems, interests,
> preferences, and ideas.

Unfortunately, it is at this point that most theories about relating to people break down. Theories tend to focus on roles or functions rather than on persons. We hear a lot about these relationships: boss/worker, management/labor, salesperson/customer, company/employee, parent/child, husband/wife, or teacher/student.

But people don't want to be treated as workers or laborers or customers or employees or parents or teenagers. People want to be treated as individuals with unique needs, desires, problems, interests, preferences, and ideas. We respond positively to those people who respect our personhood and negatively to those who treat us as a number or a category.

Anyone who sets about to relate successfully with people must start from the position that all human relationships are essentially person to person relationships. It may be that our primary contact (perhaps our only contact) with another person is in a specific role such as husband, boss, worker, customer, mother, salesperson, or student. However, our success in living and working with people will be largely determined by how much we are willing and able to look beyond those roles to see them as persons.

WHY WE NEED A SYSTEM

It's a safe bet that not only do you want to be able to get along with people but you want people to do things. You want to be able to stimulate people to act, lead them in their actions, and measure the results of their actions.

Perhaps that's why you're tired of trying to get along with people on the basis of the latest theories in vogue. Maybe you've had it with ivory-tower specialists in human relations who study people as if they were guinea pigs and offer their theories as to how to get them to do what you want them to do.

Likewise, maybe you're tired of trying a hit-or-miss approach to leading people. Perhaps you've longed to be more consistent in your successes with people, to have more satisfying relationships with those close to you, and to know how to reach out and touch others in a world that is becoming less and less personal.

If so, let me offer you a system that does not simply address the task of leadership but goes a step further to present a down-to-earth method for assuring high achievement in all human relationships.

Question 1: What Is a System?

"I have not become the King's First Minister in order to preside over the liquidation of the British Empire," said Winston Churchill shortly after his election as prime minister at the outset of World War II. Churchill's task was to lead a nation of dispirited, frightened people to arise and defend themselves against the terror of a madman (Adolf Hitler) and to preserve their way of life in the face of overwhelming odds.

To accomplish his task required inspiring hope, giving strong guidance, and marshalling all the available resources of his own people. It also included mustering massive involvement from allied nations that were strongly committed to their own people not to get involved and keeping those nations from pursuing their own selfish interests once they were involved. He was successful in both areas, and many historians have credited him with turning the tide of Nazism, Fascism, and imperialism.

Of course, it could be argued that Sir Winston Churchill was no ordinary man. Certainly he was a charismatic person, but many charismatic people have failed where he succeeded. He was a brilliant strategist, but some of the most brilliant strategists of history have failed in their hours of greatest challenge. Others will argue that England could not have stopped Hitler and Mussolini. Yet the reluctance of other nations to get involved, the degree to which many of them got involved, and the high level of their cooperation stand as a tribute to Churchill's outstanding leadership.

Few of us will ever be called upon to lead so many reluctant and dispirited people against such overwhelming odds as a world war, yet all of us are constantly confronted with the fact that we need a lot of help from others if we are to reach our goals. Wouldn't it be great to have a system that would enable us to get the maximum out of every relationship?

Sometimes people are turned off by the word *system* because it has come to mean a cold, faceless organization that acts as a barrier to reaching our goals. We hear this feeling expressed often, "You can't beat the system."

Don't let that word system frighten you. I know it's fallen into some pretty disreputable usage lately. But, originally, it was a good, strong word with a very positive meaning. It comes from the ancient Greek word *systema*, which means "to combine" or "to pull together."

But the problem is not that a system exists; rather the problem is that the *wrong* system controls too much human activity. So, what is the *right* system?

For our purposes, let's use the following definition: A *system* is an organized approach to planning, setting in motion, and guiding harmonious relationships to achieve desired results.

I like to think of a human system as a *synergy*, a combining of independent persons to obtain a higher level of achievement than all of them acting alone could reach. Simply stated, it's a way of working with people to get things done.

Question 2: What Should We Require of a System?

Listed below are seven criteria for the right system of relating to others:

1. *People-oriented*. It must start with an adequate appraisal of the value of people and take into account limitations and strengths, individuality, and needs, desires, and preferences. It must bring out the best traits and deal effectively with the worst.
2. *Simple and easy to learn*. Relating to people can be complicated enough without adding to the problems of implementing and managing a complex system nobody can understand.
3. *Practical and effective*. People need to feel free to make

mistakes as part of learning a system. More emphasis should be placed on training and coaching than on judging and disciplining.

4. *Goal-directed.* Human relationships never stand still. A desirable system will move those relationships toward the goals we desire to reach with other people.

5. *Adaptable.* It must be able to cover a wide range of relationships, situations, and environments, and it must be flexible enough to adapt to changing situations.

6. *Confidence-inspiring.* A workable system does not leave us helpless victims of the actions, attitudes, and whims of everyone around us. It puts us in position to act positively in any situation.

7. *Compatible.* The more a system agrees with the morals, personality, and principles that guide our lives, the more effective and lasting it will be.

The system I have described is the Dynamic Responsiveness System. I will outline it in the next chapter and develop it throughout the book. The Dynamic Responsiveness System meets all the preceding criteria. In fact, it surpasses them with flying colors. Further, it is not based upon high-sounding theories but has been forged by real-life events. Its underlying principles have been tested and proven over many centuries, in almost every culture of the world. It has worked effectively for many of the most outstanding leaders of history, and it will work for you.

For many years now, I've used this approach in my business, personal, family, and spiritual life. I can tell you from experience, it works. Since I can't wait to share it with you, let's go on to the next chapter.

THREE

Why a Systems Approach Works with People

One of the hardest changes I've ever had to face was shifting my management style from that of an entrepreneur to that of a professional manager.

As long as our company was small and employed only a few people, I could keep track of everything, stay in touch with everybody, and make things happen pretty much as I wanted them to happen. But as the company grew, things changed. More and more people were operating in different locations with a wide variety of clients. And small mistakes began to cost big bucks.

I had worked for large corporations before I started the company, and I had seen how easy it was for a company to become more important than its people. I had also seen how easy it was for automation to dehumanize the workplace and make people feel like machines. I wanted neither for our company or its employees. Yet our opportunities were expanding, and our tasks were becoming more complex. I was overworked. I knew I had to start developing people I could trust to act for me, cultivating people to whom I could delegate important tasks, and devising systems that could make the routine happen automatically. I needed to free myself to concentrate on the growth potential and deal with the unusual.

The more I thought about it, the more awesome the task

became. How could I stand by (and sacrifice immediate results) while key people gained management development experiences (which would produce long-term gains)? How could I watch mistakes happen and not step in as rescuer?

Although I had studied management techniques in gaining my Masters in Business Administration and had attended many seminars on the subject, and although I had seen many approaches to management, nothing seemed to offer the dynamic kind of leadership I wanted for the company or my personal life.

Company-oriented approaches with their idolization of profits seemed too insensitive. Sure, I wanted to make money, but not at the expense of sacrificing people. The task-oriented approaches had some appeal, but even they were not sensitive enough to people for me. I wanted results, but I also cared about people. This chapter discusses (1) my search for a system; (2) God's systems approach to the universe; (3) guiding principles for a viable system; (4) and the basis of all the principles.

MY SEARCH FOR A SYSTEM

Down deep inside, I believed there was a systems approach to working with people that would produce results, would enable me to achieve my goals, and would enable me to inspire others to become high achievers. A tall order! (If you read my book *Peak Performance Principles for High Achievers*, you know that I constantly set high goals for myself and with the people around me.) I knew that the system I envisioned would have to be *dynamic*—powerful and constantly moving toward progressively higher intermediate goals. And, since one of my most basic philosophies of life is that goals matter only as they relate to people, I knew the system would have to be people-oriented. It would have to enable me to realize my potential in all areas of responsibility in my life, which included my relationship to God, my wife, my children, my career, my finances, my recreational pursuits, my community, my nation, and my fellow human beings. That way, there would be no weak links and no regrets—only the synergistic effect of all the areas fitting together into a powerful, wonderful whole.

During that time, I had become a committed Christian and had begun to study the Bible. In its pages I discovered the greatest teacher of dynamic human relationships who had ever lived on this earth—Jesus.

Jesus took a small band of twelve ordinary people and, after only three years, charged them with the most important enterprise in human history. The eleven who made it through His training program went on to change the course of the world.

I examined the underlying principles Jesus used to inspire His followers to such high achievement and discovered them to be the most practical truths ever revealed for guiding human relationships—whether for business dealings, for personal life, for social activity, or simply for ordinary daily contact with other people.

Oh, I had heard businessmen say, "I run my business by the golden rule," or "I try to be honest in all my dealings with people." But what I saw involved infinitely more than clichés. Looking at what goes on under the guise of "golden rule management" and "honest dealings," I realized why Jesus was considered revolutionary in His day, and why He would be considered radical in our day. Jesus' principles call for a major overhaul of our most basic nature and requires that we value people above everything but God.

GOD'S SYSTEMS APPROACH TO THE UNIVERSE

Now, some people may not think that Jesus' approach to working with people is a system. But the idea of a systems approach to everything originated with God. He is more organized than any of His creatures.

He created a solar system, inside a galaxy, inside a universe, which is beyond all human comprehension. Everything in our universe operates so systematically that we can predict to the thousandth of a second the movements of heavenly bodies. He designed the human body, which contains vital life support systems that operate in precision to keep us going. Does it seem farfetched that God devised a system for the relationships of human beings to one another?

The Bible is a system of divine principles that enables us to apply what we know about God to the daily experience of living and dealing with other people.

First, let's take a look at some of those underlying principles. Then we'll see how it all works out into a practical system for tapping into people power.

GUIDING PRINCIPLES FOR A VIABLE SYSTEM

The basic principles Jesus outlines in His teachings have been the guiding force behind some of the greatest leaders the world has ever known. Abraham Lincoln was a remarkable humanitarian, renowned for his fair dealings with others and his plain speaking. Martin Luther King, Jr., held that all men are brothers, and his promotion of civil rights and his denunciation of racism earned him a Nobel Peace Prize in 1964. John Wesley, the founder of Methodism, devoted his life to the service of others, not only spreading the gospel but helping the needy. To alleviate human misery, Florence Nightingale worked at the practical level of improving health and defeating disease. These principles are centuries old, yet remain the most up-to-date. Most of Jesus' teachings were given to the common people and were couched in simple terms. He often used parables (stories told to illustrate a truth), analogies, and images to convey truths so simple they could be grasped by a child, but so deep they could not be fully comprehended by a genius.

For our purposes, I've isolated seven of those principles:

Principle 1: We Express Outwardly What We Are Inside

"A good man out of the good treasure of his heart brings forth good things, and an evil man out of the evil treasure brings forth evil things," was one way Jesus expressed it (see Matthew 12:33–35).

Psychologists seem to think they have made some great new discovery with their idea that the way we treat others will be determined by the way we see ourselves. They use terms like *self-image*, *self-esteem*, and *self-concept*.

What it boils down to is that we always come from the inside out in our dealings with people. If we value money over people, it will show up in the way we treat people and in our expectations of them. If we worship success over people, we'll tend to cultivate only those people who can help us and look down on those who have little to offer. If

---

We always come from the inside out
in our dealings with people.

52

we value ourselves over other people, people will be important to us only if they are serving us in some way.

The implications are staggering. For example, this unalterable principle explains why people who are afraid inside find it hard to trust anybody, why people who think they are the center of the universe enjoy walking all over others, and why people who have a lot of anger stored up inside find it easy to give hostile response to other people.

The most basic freedom we have is the freedom to choose how we will respond to what anybody says or does to us. And what will always determine the choice we make is what's going on at the deepest levels of our lives at the moment.

Thus, if we are self-motivated, people will be important to us only to the extent that they serve us. But if our motivation comes from beyond ourselves and grows out of our love for God and other people, we will value every person we meet in our daily lives.

Ralph Waldo Emerson once said, "People seem not to realize that their opinion of the world is also a confession of character." The wisdom of these words was reaffirmed for me one early spring morning when I was jogging around the neighborhood. The fresh, clear air carried the aroma of newly budding trees and flowers, and I was really enjoying the wonders of the season. As I passed by a woman on the sidewalk, I smiled and said, "Beautiful day, isn't it?" "Yeah," she replied, "but it won't last."

Principle 2: What We Give Is What We Get

"Whatever a man sows, that he will also reap," says Galatians 6:7. This principle runs through all of Jesus' teachings and His dealings with people.

The principle is so universal that it can be applied to a wide variety of subjects and actions. If we value people, we

If we value people, we will be valued;
if we don't, we won't.

will be valued; if we don't, we won't. It's that simple. If we want to be treated well, we've got to treat others well. If we want to be respected, we must respect others. If we want others to be fair and honest with us, we have to be fair and honest with others. If we want to be loved, we have to love others.

I know it doesn't always seem to work out that way. Sometimes we treat others as we'd like to be treated and they walk all over us. But the principle is so deeply rooted in God's system that, sooner or later, getting what we give always comes back to either haunt us or make us joyful.

This idea will be developed more fully later, but here I want to tell you about two people who clearly illustrate this principle. Greg and Becky Johnson spent two years living in a tent as they followed the nomadic Maasai tribe of Kenya. They chose to build trust and a relationship with the Maasai by learning firsthand the language and customs before they began their missionary ministry. The Maasai gradually accepted them, and their ministry is now flourishing. My wife and I visited Greg and Becky while we were in Africa on a mountain-climbing and game-viewing safari. We learned that twelve local tribal leaders had been converted and baptized and they were now being trained to evangelize their individual tribes. The Johnsons are really beginning to reap what they have sowed.

Principle 3: What We Use Grows; What We Don't Use We Lose

In Luke 19:11-26, Jesus illustrated this principle with the parable of the talents in which three people were rewarded on the basis of what they did with what they had been given.

If taken seriously, this concept alone could revolutionize American industry, revitalize our whole economy, and rejuvenate failing families. What we lose every day in wasted human potential, untapped creativity, and unmotivated talent could easily feed all the world's hungry and solve our most overwhelming problems, such as the high incidence of criminal activities, the muddle of mediocrity on the job and in the home, the pain and suffering caused by many stress and frustration related diseases, the unbelievably high illiteracy rate, and the deplorable standard of living endured by many people.

The worker who is stuck in a nowhere job, doing mindless tasks, for no reason but money costs us more than we could ever calculate. Each of us as individuals and society as a whole pay the price. Too often this lackadaisical worker turns out a product that seems to be more and more expensive but more and more shoddy. Poor workmanship means higher and higher repair bills (and frustration levels). Added to that, we have to consider the worth of what is lost in unused human abilities and capabilities. But to tap in to the human resources available would require a significant change in the ways we think about and act toward those who work for us and with us. Private enterprise has done more to utilize human potential than any other economic system, yet few of us have even begun to make the most of this potential.

The use-it-or-lose-it principle implies that our greatest challenge in reaching full personal potential as creatures made in the image of God is enabling others to reach their full potential. The best investment we can make in high achievement for ourselves is to inspire and enable others to become high achievers.

For this reason, supervisors from industrial plants around the country spend two weeks going through educational, motivational, and technical housekeeping training at our company's training center in Indianapolis. They spend over half their time gaining "hands-on" experience because we take seriously the saying, "You can't supervise anyone in something you haven't done, just as you can't come back from a place you've never been before."

Classroom instruction is important, but the best instruction in the world cannot build the confidence and skills that can be gained through actual performance of a task. A few years ago when I took a four-day course in high-performance race car driving, I learned that the key to driving for high performance is to do it. The classroom instruction I received before I got onto the track helped me know what I was supposed to do in certain situations and I was safe and successful when I did what I had been told to do. But I had to use their instruction through my experience to become confident and skilled. That is the way to be effective!

Principle 4: True Greatness Is Spelled S-e-r-v-i-c-e

"He who is greatest among you, let him be as the younger, and he who governs as he who serves," Jesus said in Luke 22:26. What a radical concept! Everything in our business and social structure says just the opposite: The servant is the lowest person on the social scale. And anybody who is somebody has people stumbling all over themselves in their efforts to serve.

> Those who distort the golden rule to say
> "those who have the gold, rule"
> eventually find that the only place they rule
> is in the kingdom of self.

Maybe this explains why the term "customer service" has become a too-common joke in retailing, why some people would rather stand in an unemployment compensation line than look for a job, why some employees only work when the boss is looking.

When the goal of a people shifts from serving to being served, it's not long until it becomes everybody for himself or herself. The man who refuses to assume any responsibility for work about the house and insists on being waited on by other family members; the woman who won't be on any committees unless she's to be the chairperson; the youngster who doesn't want to join the team because a key position is not guaranteed and some time must be spent on the bench—these are some of the people in need of a proper understanding about service to others.

The greatness-through-service principle says that our task is to give freely of ourselves to the people we work with, the people we live with, and the people we encounter everywhere we go. Those who distort the golden rule to say "those who have the gold, rule" eventually find that the only place they rule is in the kingdom of self.

It's this simple; in working with people, if we want to be great, we must serve others. If we give freely of ourselves, everything in heaven says this giving will come back to us many times over.

A manager in our company told me about an individual whose service to others changed the attitude of many people. Willie had held the ignoble title of "Mop Boy" for several years; that meant he was the one who cleaned up in emergencies around the plant.

When we were hired to manage this facility's housekeeping operations, Willie's title was changed to "Houseman." After all, how professional can one feel being Mop Boy? Positive names not only identify the job but also set expectations of how others respond to the person in that position.

Along with his new title, Willie received professional training and new equipment. Because he had difficulty reading, his supervisor in the housekeeping department had to help him with directions and new job schedules. He would carefully listen to them and then proceed to do an excellent day's work. From then on, the department manager would respond to calls for a Mop Boy by explaining, "There aren't any. But I will send one of my staff of trained housekeeping professionals to take care of the situation."

Eventually, the calls for the Mop Boy were replaced by requests for the Houseman. And a resurrection of personal and departmental pride accompanied this change. Soon the department was recognized for its outstanding performance. Bolstered by his new and growing confidence, Willie became a true professional in his service responsibilities, and he also completed the requirements for high school. Currently, he is serving as a shift supervisor, ably leading others out of the Mop Boy mentality.

Principle 5: Unity Brings Results

"Every kingdom divided against itself is brought to desolation, and every city or house divided against itself will not stand," Jesus said in Matthew 12:25.

Unity runs like a thread through everything God does.

Jesus went so far as to say, "Love your enemies . . . do good to those who hate you" (Matthew 5:44). Now that's a big assignment, but those who take it seriously find that it pays big dividends in working with people.

"It has always seemed to me that the best symbol of common sense was the bridge," said Franklin D. Roosevelt. No task of the person who wants to work with people will require more constant effort or greater creativity than building bridges to those who choose to be your adversaries.

The unity principle implies that a loving, accepting, and cooperative attitude toward everybody we encounter will lead to great effectiveness in getting things done. It suggests that status distinctions, such as labor/management, child/parent, lay/clergy, us/them, good guy/bad guy, are too limited and must give way to walking arm in arm. It also suggests that, in every area of life, those who would choose to be our enemies should find us constantly trying to win them over.

When I was growing up in southern Indiana, a bunch of us would walk down a railroad track to the White River on hot summer days. We discovered three ways to walk the track: (1) on the ties, (2) between the ties, and (3) on the rails. Have you ever tried to walk on the rails? It's not as easy as it sounds. How far do you think you could go before you would fall off? A few feet? A few yards?

What if I could show you how to walk a mile without falling off? This is how it works: You stand on one rail, and I stand on the other. Then you wrap your hand around my arm, and I wrap my hand around your arm. Then down the track we go, joined together for the adventure.

That's the essence of working with people. Walking hand in hand, arm in arm, side by side with people who are great and who inspire you, and also with people you want to inspire to be great—at work, in your home, at your church, wherever you serve.

Principle 6: Responsiveness Grows from a Sense of Responsibility

In the parable of the good Samaritan (Luke 10:25–37), Jesus makes it quite clear that each one of us is responsible for the well-being of the people around us. It is only when we are aware of that responsibility that we can be as responsive to others as needed for effectiveness.

Commitment is a big part of any relationship whether it's marriage, friendship, or business. Our natural tendency is to think about what others should bring to that relationship, not what we should bring. Race-car drivers know the importance of working with their cars and of being sensitive and alert to everything that is going on within them, from the tires to the throttle. Drivers must be prepared at all times for the emergency situations that can develop in a machine performing at peak levels. If individuals can be this committed to maintaining a relationship with an inanimate object, how much more committed should they be to work with one another in human relationships to achieve peak performance living! Sensitivity and alertness to the needs of others, awareness of an individual's potential, and preparation to cope with life's emergencies are some things we can bring to a relationship.

The principle of responsibility implies that if we are going to work effectively with people we must express that responsibility through responsiveness to their needs, to their interests, and even to their very personhood.

A seventy-five-year-old grandmother admirably exemplified this principle. Knowing that the effects of a malignancy would soon end her life, she summoned her large family to her hospital bedside. Sons and daughters, their spouses and their children crowded into her room. She acknowledged the presence of each one and then spoke to them all, "For seventy-five years I've been modeling for you how to live like a Christian. Now I'm going to show you how to die like one."

Principle 7: Perseverance Produces Results

The parable of the persistent widow, in Luke 18:1-8, makes it clear that results come to those who persevere—who keep on keeping on. The woman in the story had asked an ungodly judge for relief from a person who was trying to take advantage of her helplessness. The judge refused to act in her behalf, but she kept on showing up every time he went to court and pleading with him to do something. Finally, he said, "Though I do not fear God nor regard man, yet because this widow troubles me I will avenge her, lest by her coming she weary me." Of course Jesus' point was that if perseverance pays off with the ungodly, we can be sure that a loving God will answer those who persevere with Him.

This principle, however, is not limited to prayer. Again and again it showed up in His teachings. Among other things, it includes the idea that if we consistently pursue even the most difficult people to work with, we can eventually win them over. For example, the parable of the prodigal son (Luke 15) is more about a loving father who was willing to give his son a second chance than about a boy who ran away from home.

The principle of perseverance suggests that when a relationship with anyone around us is not good, we can turn it around through persistent and untiring efforts and understanding.

On the morning of my first attempt at a twenty-six-mile marathon, I had a sinking feeling by the time we had gone only a mile and a half. Behind me were only twenty or thirty of the eleven hundred runners. The rest were in front of me, as far as I could see. I began to question whether to stick with my predetermined pace of an eight-and-a-half-minute mile. About that time another runner came alongside me and asked if this was my first marathon. He had seen me looking back and thought he might offer some encouragement. He assured me that if I maintained my pace, I would pass half the people ahead of us. I did just that and came in 575th.

If I had tried to run that race without a reasonable pace, without a strategy designed to help me finish successfully, and without the perseverance to stick to that pace and that strategy, I know I would have never finished. The real race of life is more like a marathon than a hundred-yard dash, but many people fail to develop the perseverance that running the longer race requires. Giving up on a relationship—with a family member, a colleague, a friend—is certainly much simpler than sticking with it and trying to make it work, but when it does work, you will be glad that you persisted.

THE BASIS OF ALL THE PRINCIPLES

As powerful as each of those seven principles is, they all rest upon one foundation—the commandment to "love your neighbor as yourself" (Romans 13:9). All the principles are nothing more than further explanations of the one basic idea that we are to love others as we love ourselves.

Isn't it interesting that most major psychological studies done in our high-tech age point to the very needs these principles address so forcefully? Child-rearing experts are proclaiming how important it is for our children to grow up with a positive self-image. Counselors are telling their single clients that part of the emptiness of their lives stems from their unwillingness to invest themselves in lasting relationships. On and on it goes. The adversarial climate in our industries cripples product quality and productivity. Behind-the-scenes back scratching and budget padding continue to increase the costs of government.

As I studied the seven principles and their underlying basis, I knew that any system of managing my company or my personal life had to take them into account.

What's more, I began to catch a glimpse of just how dynamic and powerful these principles are. They contained the very seeds of the kind of relationships I wanted for the people with whom I live and work. The system began to emerge.

C H A P T E R

FOUR

Why the Dynamic Responsiveness System Gets Results

Dynamic Responsiveness: A system for compelling people to give their best efforts to achieve mutually attractive goals. A way of planning, organizing, and leading people for high achievement in families, businesses, and corporations.

The Dynamic Responsiveness System contains four practical components that are simple, easy to learn and implement, and easy to remember.

1. *Value people* (including yourself) above everything but God.
2. *Give to people* what you want to get from people.
3. *Make cooperation a way of life.*
4. *Keep doing it!*

That's simple enough, isn't it? Actually, at first glance it may seem too simplistic to meet the personal and organizational needs of today's complex world. But I remember my grandfather, a teacher all his life, saying more than once, "If you can't say something simple, you don't understand it well enough." There's more here than is first apparent. You'll see what I mean when we begin talking about how it all works.

In fact, the Dynamic Responsiveness System is so comprehensive that we will spend the remainder of the book explaining how you can take advantage of it in working with people. Let's begin by taking a look at how it all works, then we'll turn our attention to how you can become a dynamic influence by becoming increasingly responsive to other people.

HOW DYNAMIC RESPONSIVENESS WORKS

The most basic idea behind Dynamic Responsiveness is that you gain power with people by responding positively to their needs, interests, and concerns. It means that people will give their very best to a person, an organization, or even a cause, that is responsive to their best interests.

The terrorist suicide bombings of the American military barracks and embassy in Beirut demonstrate just how powerful this idea is. Misguided as those Muslims might have been, they gladly gave their lives for a cause (their religion) they believed was the answer to their greatest needs in this life and in the life to come.

Dictators like Fidel Castro, Juan Peron, and Moammar Khadafy hold whole nations of people in their iron grip for decades. How? By sheer power alone? No one person is that strong. They convince enough people that their government is in their best interest. The people are so convinced of this that they are willing to lay their lives on the line to defend the dictator's regime. When people become

> You gain power with people
> by responding positively to their
> needs, interests, and concerns.

disenchanted enough to band together, a revolution occurs, and a new regime is instituted. Responsiveness is a powerful force in motivating people.

The illustrations used so far point to a disturbing fact: The power of responsiveness can be misused with devastating results. Jim Jones led over 900 people to kill themselves by calling them his children and convincing them their liberators were their enemies. People who resort to such tactics as deception, false hopes, and manipulation usually use responsiveness.

Now, I don't want you to become a Jim Jones or a Fidel Castro so that you can work more effectively with people. I assume that if your motives had not been good, the section on Jesus' principles in the preceding chapter would have turned you off, and you would not have read this far.

Responsiveness, however, contains a trap that even people with the best of motives can fall into. Most of us tend to promise more than we can deliver. When we do, we raise (consciously or unconsciously) false hopes in those we would lead.

For example, I believe America has fallen into the trap of holding out false hopes. Our welfare system may be a genuine attempt to be responsive to the needs of the underprivileged, but some individuals have become too dependent on it and, as a result, have given up trying to live any other way. Many young people fall prey to the claims of how they can become instant successes; attend this college, get that degree, do this, learn that, and you're sure to be a big winner before you're twenty-five. They often become disillusioned when they realize that they can't accomplish great feats in a short period of time. And, as much as I believe in our private enterprise system, its advertising is built around wish-fulfillment buying. Toothpaste as sex appeal, deodorant as a career strategy, and beer as a means to camaraderie raise expectations that those products cannot fulfill.

The Dynamic Responsiveness System will enable you to avoid those pitfalls and to exercise a powerful influence on the lives of others for their own good. But I feel compelled to caution you that the system must be taken as a whole and used not only for your good, but for the good of others too.

Let's take a closer look at each of the components and what it implies for practical daily working with people.

VALUE PEOPLE ABOVE EVERYTHING BUT GOD

In business schools we are not taught to value people. There the emphasis is on money—how to sell more goods and services, how to make higher profits by getting more people to do more work for less pay, and how to build big organizations around money-making goals.

Dynamic Responsiveness starts with valuing people above money, above organizations, above machines, above material things, above an immaculate house, above vacations or holidays, above TV and movies, above busy schedules, above everything but God. Then goals become people-centered, organizations become vehicles for serving people, and money becomes a commodity to be used by people—not vice versa. But what does that mean?

Guideline 1: Place the Proper Value upon Yourself

You can value others properly only when you have your own value in proper perspective. How do you do that? Certainly not by tallying up your assets and subtracting your liabilities, not by estimating your worth by your authority, or your recognition, or your achievements, or your status, not by any of the common methods of keeping score.

> You can value others properly
> only when you have your own value
> in proper perspective.

Look for clues to your worth as a human being in such realities as these:

- You were created by God.
- You were made in God's image, and you can't find a better mold than that.
- You have a rightful place in the universe, but not at its center.
- You have just as much value as, but no more than, any other human being.
- You have been given fantastic abilities that can be useful to you and others as you discover and develop them.
- You have limitations, and accepting them will give you peace of mind and enable you to relate more openly to other people.

What it all boils down to is that you accept yourself as you are, and go from there. You are created; you are not the creator. That means you don't have to be perfect, just responsive to the One who is perfect. And it means you don't have to try to carry the world on your shoulders like Atlas, the character from Greek mythology.

When you can value yourself as much as, but no more than, any other person, you're ready to face up to the second guideline.

Guideline 2: Accept Others as They Are

That word *accept* bothers some of us because we confuse it with the words *agree* and *approve*. *To agree* means "to be in harmony with," and we will meet many people whose ideas, motivations and actions we cannot agree with. *To approve* means "to deem satisfactory," and many actions and attitudes we simply cannot deem satisfactory.

But *to accept* means something altogether different. It means "to receive graciously." Wow! What a powerful concept! We can accept people, warts and all!

This idea opens the door for you to accept people despite their liabilities—their bad attitudes and actions, their limitations, and their problems. It means you can work with them without expecting more from them than they can, or want, to give.

More positively, it means you can graciously receive the gifts they bring. You can trade your abilities, resources, and good will for their abilities, resources, and good will—and everyone will be richer for the exchange.

It's a far different vantage point from trying to bribe people into doing what they don't want to do, or coercing them to yield to pressure, or cramming them into a situation that serves only your ends.

Guideline 3: Value People Properly—Utilize People and Use Things

The word *using* carries with it the negative concept of expending without regard for giving anything in return. Thus, many individuals who would lead others simply use people.

But *utilizing* has the connotation of taking full advantage of what is freely offered and leaving the one who is the giver better off. It means your great challenge in working

> Making winners of other people
> is a game you simply cannot lose.

with people is to make winners out of all. Making winners of other people is to make a winner out of you! Making winners of other people is a game you simply cannot lose.

The biblical principle of stewardship includes being held accountable for all your resources. No resource has greater value, nor requires greater stewardship, than the talents offered by family members, coworkers, customers, or people who simply walk through the doors.

A tendency today is to value things and use people. But when people are valued above machines, gadgets, and material possessions, things become nothing more than tools people use in their efforts to realize their full potential. Thus, all the inventions of our high-tech environment can serve to liberate people rather than enslave them. The Dynamic Responsiveness System can help you adapt to today's technological advances as well as tomorrow's, which promise to be even more sophisticated.

Guideline 4: Value People by Acting Responsibly Toward All People, Not Just Those Who Have Something You Want

Systems that put the self at the center of the universe urge you to spend time and energy only on those people who can make you successful and to approach every relationship with the objective of getting only what you want out of it—to "do unto others, then split." Not so with Dynamic Responsiveness.

> To carry another's load is
> to devalue that person by
> making him or her dependent.

In God's system of valuing people, there are no "little" people or "big" people. We stand alike on level ground.

As one who values people, I have the obligation to act responsively toward the clerk who takes my money, the officer who writes me a ticket, and even the bum on the street, as well as to the corporate president who signs my check. Taken seriously, this concept alone could revolutionize the American system of commerce and trade and revitalize our personal relationships.

Now, all this does not mean that I must assume my neighbor's responsibility. I like the old Eastern proverb, "If a man comes to you hungry one day, give him a fish; if he comes back hungry the next day, teach him how to fish." Indeed, to carry another's load is to devalue that person by making him or her dependent. The dominant trend, however, has been more toward being unresponsive than toward being too responsive.

Guideline 5: Keep It All in Balance

Admittedly, the question of how much value to place on each person you work with is a toughie. Yet whether you will respond to or react against people is determined by your appraisal of their value.

If, on the one hand, you see others as having *more* value than you have, you will either look up to them and admire them, or you will resent them and look for ways to cut them down to size. Even if you look up to them, you tend to become dependent, or to be overly solicitous, or to expect too much. Nobody can measure up to the expectations of another when placed on a pedestal.

On the other hand, if you see others as having *less* value than you have, you tend to look down on them. You may treat them with scorn, or ignore them, or even become openly hostile toward them.

Either assessment—overvaluing or undervaluing—can make you defensive toward other people. You become afraid of what they might do to you, then you set about to defend yourself against the motives you have ascribed to them. This is one of the most common sources of conflict in human relationships.

Love demands that you assess all persons as having value equal to yours and that you remain responsive to them even when they are not responsive to you.

Responding carries with it the positive idea of moving favorably toward another person. *Reacting* carries with it the idea of resisting or backing away from another. Whether you respond or react will be determined by your assessment of the person in question.

For example, identical twin girls grew up with an alcoholic father. When they reached adulthood, one twin became an alcoholic, the other an abstainer. The sisters were interviewed by a psychologist. The psychologist asked the first twin why she became an alcoholic. She responded, "Well, what do you expect from the daughter of an alcoholic?" In a separate session, the psychologist asked the second twin why she became an abstainer. She said, "Well, what do you expect from the daughter of an alcoholic?"

What happens to us in life is not nearly so important as how we respond to it. That's what the Dynamic Responsiveness System is all about. It is an orderly way to choose how we will respond to all persons and any circumstance. We can choose to respond, rather than to react.

And that leads us to the second component of the Dynamic Responsiveness System.

GIVE TO PEOPLE WHAT YOU WANT TO GET

If you want loyalty from people, give loyalty; if you want service, give service; if you want recognition, give recognition; if you want rewards, give rewards; if you want love, give love and make yourself more lovable. Whatever you want people to do for you, do for other people.

> We can choose to respond,
> rather than to react.

In this age of the glorified self, the second component might cause some readers to choke and drop the book. It goes against all the brainwashing of our present culture. Schools, media advertising, magazine articles, and books all constantly tell us that those who are most aggressive get what they want out of life. And a lot of evidence supports that idea. We do tend to be submissive to aggressive people. Sometimes people who walk all over others get promotions because their superiors feel they're tough enough to get the job done.

Yet there is a universal law that says that giving is the way to get more of what you want. For example, one of the oldest principles of business is that if you want to be successful, find a need and fill it. Countless entrepreneurs have done just that.

Sooner or later, we reap what we sow.

If we want our children to pay attention to us when we're old, we must pay attention to them when they're young and continue to show concern for them as they pass from adolescence to adulthood. If we want our children to feel secure, we parents must show love to each other. If we want sincere friendship, we must find the needs of others and fill them. If we want respect from our coworkers, we must show respect for them.

The late Howard Hughes was one of the most powerful men who ever lived. Documents discovered after his death revealed that he believed his god—money—could buy any man, including the president of the United States. Not only was he proven wrong, but his overwhelming fear of people and diseases forced him to lead the last few years of his life as a recluse and to die totally alone. An individual who spends his life selfishly ends up with only himself.

Those who try to intimidate others into fulfilling their desires might get some cooperation (especially if they have the upper hand), but they will not be able to get people to give their best. The manager, teacher, parent, or spouse who continually resorts to shape-up-or-ship-out tactics may have some short-term success but will never win respect, admiration, and affection, things that really matter in the long run.

Believe me, eventually it always works out: The more you give, the more you receive. The rewards may not always be money or recognition or even the respect of some people you value too highly. But you will have power with people.

But what does it mean to give what you want to get? Let's take a look at some of the ways we express it in real life.

Action 1: Serve Those You Would Lead

Most of the effective leaders I know work a lot harder than the people they lead. They know that they can only expect followers to give their best when they, themselves give their best. But they have become responsive leaders because they give so freely of themselves. They have learned that those who give their best, receive the best. On the home front and in business, these people motivate others by being examples.

Does this mean you become a responsive leader by working yourself to death to satisfy the whims of self-centered people? Usually, it means precisely the opposite. When you value yourself and others equally, you give freely those things that are appropriate for a leader to give—even a loving kick in the seat of the pants. Since you don't want to be burdened by an unhealthy dependence as a leader, don't provoke it in a follower. You give what you determine to be your best, not what self-centered people demand from you.

My clients saw a lot of me in the early years of our management and training business. As it grew, however, I pulled myself out of the day-to-day operations and transferred the mantle of authority to other managers. I trusted my managers to do a good job and satisfy our clients, and the clients and I were not disappointed.

A senior minister may feel himself being pulled in all directions because everyone in the congregation wants his personal attention. In this situation he would do well to recognize the impossibility of meeting such demands and call upon the other members of his staff.

Do you know the difference between a politician and a statesman? A politician kowtows to the demands of the most valued constituents (usually the rich and powerful) and tries to sway the masses into thinking they are best served by the interests of the few. But the statesman tries faithfully to serve the best interests of all his or her constituents, even when to do so is not popular.

Another issue is involved here. Life does not balance its books at the end of every day, and you don't always receive from the same people to whom you give. The process of reaping what you have sown may take years, and the harvest may come from fields where you did not sow. But be assured, sooner or later, you will receive in proportion to what you have given.

Last year my ten-year-old son asked if he could start mowing our lawn so that he could earn money for a new bike. I was thrilled with his initiative, and I knew it would be a good opportunity to teach him the value of work.

There was only one problem. Our mower, though in good condition, proved to be too hard for him to start or to change the bag. So I bought a new six-hundred-dollar mower with the latest convenience features, and I showed him how to operate it. Economically it makes no sense to spend that amount so a youngster can earn seven dollars each time he mows the lawn, but developmentally it does. If he knows that I will encourage him and help him in this endeavor, he knows that he can count on me in other areas of life, too. And he also gains independence by working toward his goal of the new bicycle instead of asking me to give it to him.

Companies and institutions as well as individuals must have vision to anticipate what will be needed and then be willing to invest time, talent, and money to satisfy that need. Otherwise, growth will be stifled.

Shortly after graduating with my master's degree in business administration, I worked for a major meat-packing company, and the president of the firm put this principle into action. He assigned me the task of preparing a proposal to justify the addition of a third bacon cutting and packaging line. I enthusiastically gathered facts and figures, determined to put together a masterpiece of ingenuity and creativity.

But a strange thing happened. I could find no viable reason to have a third line because the two production lines we had were not being used to capacity. I presented my conclusions to the president only to be informed that the board had already granted approval and the order for the machinery had been placed. I was stunned!

He proceeded to explain the reason for that decision. He said, "John, if we don't put in a third line now, we will never grow any bigger. Our sales force won't try to sell more because they know we can't supply more. I can't let that type of thinking hamper this firm's potential. Soon I'll announce to the sales and marketing people the plans to put in a third bacon line, and I'll also inform them that we expect to increase our sales accordingly."

The sales of that company increased dramatically during the next few months and years—all because of the president's vision and his willingness to serve those he would lead.

Action 2: Set Goals Others Want to Reach

If you want to experience high achievement, choose people-oriented goals. The more compatible your goals are to the goals of the people with whom you want to relate, the more people will give of themselves in reaching those goals, and the more they will enjoy the process.

The best way to explain that is to give an illustration from my first major experience in mountain climbing. Alfons Franzen, my German-Swiss guide when I climbed the Matterhorn, is a master leader. He had experienced what I had only studied, he had been where I wanted to go, and he gave freely of himself to help me reach a goal that really mattered to me. Because I believed he could help me reach a goal I really wanted to reach, I would have done anything he told me to do.

To show you just how compelling his leadership was, let me share one brief experience. Once, when my hands were freezing from the extreme cold and were becoming numb, I stopped climbing.

The tips of my fingers began to sting and then burn. Was this frostbite? I took off my gloves, and I blew into my cupped hands again and again, trying to restore the feeling.

"Climb!" came the command from above. But I kept blowing into my hands. "What are you doing down there, John?" Alfons demanded.

"I'm blowing on my hands, Alfons!" I shouted back.

"We don't have time for that. Climb!" he barked like a drill sergeant.

"But Alfons, my hands—they're freezing!" I pleaded.

"Beat 'em on the rocks!" he commanded.

Was he serious? Beat them on the rocks? Do you know what I did? I started beating them on the rocks. Within a minute, I'd beaten the feeling back into my hands.

"Now, continue to beat your hands on the rocks the rest of the way up. Do you understand me?" he yelled.

"Yes, sir," I said humbly.

I would have done whatever my guide told me to do because he was leading me toward a goal that had become my personal dream. That's compelling leadership! He was leading by responding to my desires and needs.

MAKE COOPERATION A WAY OF LIFE

Cooperation begets cooperation. All of us have seen people who try to "motivate" through intimidation. When something goes wrong, their first priority is to fix the blame—ostensibly to assure it won't happen again. A primary method of the intimidator is the old-fashioned "chewing out."

But let me ask you a question. How do you react to a chewing out—especially when you get it with other people present? Do you want to respond by giving your best? Or would you rather give your intimidator a piece of your mind and walk out?

More often than not, the person who resorts to such tactics is merely taking advantage of his or her position to vent anger. Unfortunately, this has become a way of life for too many people. For four decades psychologists have been telling us the healthiest thing we can do is to let our anger out, express what we feel. "When you express your anger, it goes away," they have told us.

More recently, however, a number of studies have shown that precisely the opposite happens. It has been indicated that the more vehemently people expressed their anger, the more angry they became. Instead of defusing the emotion, expressing anger actually feeds it.

Of course, this doesn't even take into account the law of reaping and sowing. When people get chewed out, they seldom remain passive about it. They usually react in some negative way. Even if they are not in a position to let loose their wrath on the perpetrator, they find others ways to get even.

The individual delivering the ultimatum, "Do what you're told," may find that people do exactly that, whether the instruction is right or wrong. The plight of one supervisor shows what can happen in such cases. Sam discovered inefficient procedures being used to refinish the tile floors in the plant. When he tried to suggest improvements, Dick, his immediate supervisor, not only refused to listen but also chewed him out and told him to do as he was told.

Instead of defusing the emotion,
expressing anger actually feeds it.

When Sam reported the events to the rest of the floor crew, they agreed to follow Dick's instructions to the letter, even if they knew he was wrong.

One day Dick mistakenly scheduled the crew to strip and wax the floor in a section of the purchasing department that was carpeted. The crew did strip and wax the floor, but they had to tear up the carpet to do it. They hoped that Dick would be jolted off his high horse when he got those calls from people angry over the state of their floor.

A member of our consulting staff took a positive approach to getting people to cooperate when he was faced with a tense situation in a large health care facility. The state health inspector had cited the housekeeping department for letting excessive dust build up. As a result, the housekeeping supervisor really chewed out his people, calling them lazy and incompetent. Added to that was the less-than-pleasant attitude of other departments because the deficiency reflected on the facility as a whole. A decline in morale and effectiveness ensued, and the housekeeping staff adopted the defensive attitude that they needed more staff and more hours to solve the problem.

Our manager carefully evaluated the situation before he took any action. Then he met with the housekeeping staff. First, he tried to reinstill their confidence by reminding them of their importance in providing a safe, clean environment. Next, he praised them for the areas in which they were doing well. Then, he asked each person to identify areas that needed to be dusted; thus, he made them aware of areas they had missed while he showed them respect by asking and not telling.

Management conceded that the schedules were demanding, but there was no way to hire more people or allow more hours of work at that time. It was agreed that some new supplies would be purchased to facilitate the work. The meeting ended with a spirit of agreement, and sixty days later the state inspector gave the housekeeping department a perfect score.

There's incredible wisdom in the ancient Hebrew proverb, "A soft answer turns away wrath." Believe me, it works! We'll talk much more later about how you can use a "soft answer" to defuse a tense situation, and what a powerful tool it is.

But cooperativeness has more potential than just taking off the pressure when things get tense. Adopting a cooperative attitude toward all people can enable you to be responsive to new ideas, to help integrate new people into your organization, to attract talented people, and so much more. And it works in all directions—up, down, and sideways . . . superiors, subordinates, and peers. People you work with, live with, play with, or simply bump into want to do what you want them to do.

Let's focus briefly on ways to adopt cooperation as a way of life.

Method 1: Develop a Positive Attitude
Toward Every Person

You should develop a positive attitude toward every person you encounter in every area of life. Certainly this is part of valuing people, but it has practical implications as well.

When your attitude is unconditional, one of warm regard for all persons you meet, it helps them relax, and people at ease are able to perform better. Your positive attitude helps to build a trust bond so that other people become less defensive and more willing to cooperate.

But won't people walk all over you if you are so cooperative? Only the insecure are so defensive that they fear everyone they meet is trying to take advantage of them. For example, we have found that insecure supervisors often propose adding more people as the solution to plant housekeeping problems. Yet, in most cases, the solution is better scheduling and training. Responsive people are too busy reaching for high goals to be worried about who's going to walk all over them.

That leads me to the next implication of adopting cooperation as a way of life.

Method 2: Be Willing to Say No—Graciously

Be willing to say no when it must be said, but learn to say it graciously and with an eye to being cooperative. And smile, if appropriate. Smiling changes not only your facial expressions but your tone of voice as well.

Mary Kay Ash, in her book *Mary Kay on People Management*, tells a hypothetical story to illustrate how to do this. "A person may ask for an unreasonably high increase in salary, one that does not give the company a fair return for services rendered. 'My wife lost her job, and we have two kids in college,' an employee may plead; 'I need a raise.' A good manager will be sympathetic, but he can't always comply with even the most justifiable wants and needs of his employees," Mary Kay (as she's widely known) concludes.

This woman who has built a company employing more than 200,000 consultants and directors gave the following formula for handling such situations.

1. It is imperative that each employee be confident that no decision will be arbitrary. And so the first thing I do is to listen and then restate the question. This reassures the employee that I do indeed understand the scope of the problem.
2. I clearly list the logical reasons why his request cannot be granted.
3. I give a direct "no" statement. This is so important if you are

to build respect among people. It's not fair to expect someone else to surmise or guess your real intent.

4. And finally I try to suggest how the employee's goal may be reached by some other path. For example, to this hypothetical employee I might say, "Bill, I am truly sorry about your wife's misfortune. But you know, she may be on the threshold of a whole new career. This could be your opportunity to help her discover her real talents. God didn't have time to make a nobody; we all have the capacity for greatness. Why don't you sit down with her tonight and talk about what she would really like to accomplish next?"

Responsive leadership demands both tough-mindedness and tender-heartedness. The same is true for being a good follower, a good coworker, and a good family member. You don't have to always say yes, but you can always find a way to say no graciously and with an eye to cooperation.

Method 3: Practice Cooperation
Until It Becomes Automatic

Learn how to cooperate and practice until it becomes automatic. We learn very early in life to be uncooperative. Any parent can tell you why a child's second birthday is called the beginning of the "terrible twos." Suddenly, everything becomes "Me do it!" and "No!" and the struggle begins in earnest to determine who's in charge of the family.

For whatever reasons, many people never outgrow this uncooperative attitude. They enter adulthood (and may even spend their whole lives) wanting to do only as they wish and resenting anyone who doesn't agree with them. For example, Jack shares his idea for developing a new product with his coworker Bill, and Bill points out a few changes that he thinks would make the product more attractive to the company's managers (and to consumers).

Jack reacts angrily and resolves to never again discuss his ideas with Bill. Jack's uncooperative attitude would easily limit the effectiveness of his current idea and restrict what he and Bill might have been able to achieve together in the future.

Dynamic Responsiveness demands that you learn how to cooperate with others at all levels and in all areas of your life. It means being willing to push aside selfish motives to gain cooperation. Sometimes it even means changing, or at least not insisting upon, your opinions about the right and wrong ways to do everything.

Method 4: Bring Others in on Decisions

Practicing cooperation means that you bring others in on the decisions that affect their lives. There's an old axiom, "People support what they help create." I've found that to be true in my business, my family life, my social contacts— in every area of my life.

> A "we" decision always produces
> more cooperation than an "I" decision.

People who take charge of every situation they're thrown into very often find themselves either getting little done or doing it all themselves. But people who are responsive to the ideas, needs, and motivations of others usually discover that a "we" decision always produces more cooperation than an "I" decision.

Real estate salespeople recognize that the decision to buy comes when the family takes "psychological ownership" of the house, when the family members begin to say, "This will be my bedroom" or "This kitchen has all the features we've been talking about" or "We will really enjoy the family room with its fireplace on cold winter evenings." They each begin to feel a part of the decision to move into *this* new house.

I can't imagine a less enthusiastic group than a family on a vacation that was decided *for* them. Allowing family members to participate in choosing the destination, activities, and sights along the way will make the trip a lot more agreeable for everyone.

A sure way to make employees unhappy is to decorate their offices without consulting them. Even if some of their requests may initially seem unreasonable or unworkable, they will provide a place to begin discussions. The sales staff that has a say in setting its goals is going to work hard to live up to its own expectations. The sales manager might have specified the same goals the staff decided upon, but in the final analysis, people will feel more positive and cooperative about something in which they have participated.

Method 5: Monitor Results—Not People

Practicing cooperation means monitoring results, not people. "I like to keep close watch on my people. It's the only way I can keep them working," a manager once told me. I needed to watch for only a few minutes to see what happened when he turned his back. Activity was feverish when he was around, but the pace would slow to a near stop as soon as he was out of sight.

I don't care whose theory says you can, experience tells me you cannot bring out the best in people by looking over their shoulders. Some people will look extremely busy while accomplishing nothing; others will look very relaxed while getting a lot done. Feverish activity means nothing but that someone has raised the temperature!

When you give a lot, you can expect a lot in return. Desire is the key to all motivation, and desire can be produced only by responsiveness. When people do what you want done because you have led them to want to do it, then the function of monitoring becomes merely helping people discover more productive ways of doing their tasks.

> Desire is the key to
> all motivation, and
> desire can be produced
> only by responsiveness.

One evening before I was to address a group of top executives, the president of the company made a point of introducing himself to me. As he shook my hand, he looked straight into my eyes and said, "Mr. Noe, I've never heard of you before. But I'm paying you a lot of money to kick off this conference. You'd better be good!" He created an even greater-than-usual desire in me to do a good job, and I did my best not to disappoint him.

Method 6: Make Improvement the Goal of All Criticism

Practicing cooperation means that the goal of all criticism is improvement. Petty criticism has no place in the vocabulary of the responsive person. The responsive person gives only constructive criticism, gives it sparingly, always sandwiches it between two compliments, and never gives it in the presence of others.

Not long after I began my own business, I made a presentation to some managers of an automobile factory. I had worked hard to come up with a proposal that would meet their needs, and I felt good about it. After I finished, the group said they would think about it and let us know.

A man who worked with me had also attended the meeting, and as we walked to the car, I asked him how he thought I had done. He answered, "John, that was pretty good. You obviously knew what you were saying, but compared to what you're capable of, it was only average." Then he explained how I could improve my presentations by asking probing questions and being more sensitive to the needs of clients. I used his suggestions in the next presentation I made with him, and we closed the sale.

Now, let's take a look at the final component of the Dynamic Responsiveness System.

KEEP DOING IT!

Dynamic Responsiveness is a lifetime pursuit, a lifestyle that produces fantastic results in every area of life. But you have to keep at it.

Sincerity is one of the greatest assets any of us can have in working with people, whatever the relationship. And the only way we can demonstrate sincerity is to be sincere.

I've seen salespeople, managers, and coworkers turn on the charm and appear ever so responsive to someone they wanted to impress. But when the person they valued more highly than others left, the smile disappeared and a frown took over. Responsiveness simply cannot be turned on and off at will. People can tell the difference no matter how cleverly you try to disguise it.

You watch it! People who are responsive to harried waitresses and disgruntled clerks will be responsive in business to customers, workers, and bosses alike, and in their personal relationships with family and friends. Responsiveness becomes a way of life for these people. It shows up wherever they are, and it makes them dynamic people who can get others to do things.

Remember, the way you treat an employee is closely observed by all other employees (or one family member by the other family member). They decide whether you can be trusted on the basis of your sincerity. The assumption is that they will be treated in the same way.

Of course, some resistant people seem not to warm up to any amount of responsiveness on your part. Even with those people, however, your chances of improving the relationship rise sharply with the degree to which you keep on being responsive.

What it basically means is that you consciously decide to respond positively to any person or any situation you encounter. It means you never surrender your right to choose your response to any person.

I like the way Abraham Lincoln said it, "I will not allow any man to reduce my soul to the level of hatred."

THE LINE BENEATH THE BOTTOM LINE

What we're really talking about is love. Granted, we've been talking about a way of expressing love; but the line beneath the bottom line in all human relationships is love. And those who love others most freely become truly important to those they love. Anything else is just a sham.

Charles Mergendahl expressed it like this in his book *The Next Best Thing:*

There's only one thing in this world that's worth having. Love. L-O-V-E. You love somebody, somebody loves you. That's all there is to it. But if you don't get that, you've got nothing. So you take the next best thing. You take power or money or fame or whatever little morsel you can pick for yourself as second best.

I hope in this chapter I've convinced you that the key to having power is to love others and to express that love by being responsive. You'll find some valuable pointers in the next chapter about being responsive in an unresponsive world.

FIVE

Why You Should Be a Responsive Person in an Unresponsive World

The faster and farther we go down the road toward automation, the greater the need for responsiveness becomes, and the harder it becomes to remain responsive to people.

When you work with machines all day, are entertained by gadgets all evening, and are served everything from money to food by electronic vendors all weekend, it is difficult to remain sensitive to people—especially when the masses of other people seem to be growing less and less sensitive.

Responsive people have always found a way, however, and they always seem to be in great demand. They've learned (1) to go beyond authority to power; (2) to have a responsive state of mind; (3) to set the pace; and (4) to understand the roles of a responsive leader.

BEYOND AUTHORITY TO POWER

Maybe you've never thought about it, but there's a tremendous difference between *authority* and *power*.

One of the little gods of the status conscious is authority. The status conscious love titles, job descriptions naming all the people who answer to them, and outward displays of their importance. Somehow, they think that when they get a promotion it's as if someone has stamped AUTHORITY or IMPORTANT across their foreheads.

But the people who really get things done in this world are those who have power with other people. You'll see them in meetings saying things like:

"What would you like for me to do?"

"If that's what you need, we'll get it done!"

"Tell me about it!"

"How can we solve the problem?"

"It's okay! We'll make up for it somehow!"

"No problem! We'll find a way!"

You'll find people like this in every organization. They're the ones others turn to when they have a need. And their response to the needs of others is what gives them power. They show they care, and they get things done.

A good, sharp secretary is a prime example of such a person. Anyone who's spent very much time around businesses or other organizations knows that secretaries are unsung heroes. They know where everything is, what to do when others only stand wringing their hands, and how to work with an incredible array of people. What's more, a secretary can often set the mood for an entire office, keep customers or clients happy, and make up for a boss's mistakes.

If you think they're not powerful people, just ask salespersons who call on offices regularly. They'll tell you in a minute that keeping good working relationships with secretaries is high on their priority list. Or ask the boss whose secretary has been out sick for a couple of days. Everything can go bonkers because nobody can find or do anything.

Now I'm praising not just secretaries, although I surely want to stay in good with mine; I'm pointing up the fact that some of the most influential people have little authority but much power and that people power comes from being responsive to the needs and interests of other people.

> Some of the most influential people
> have little authority but much power.

When my son Ken was four years old, he obviously had little authority, but I discovered he knew something about people power. One Saturday morning I was listening to some salesmanship tapes on how to close a sale, and Ken was lying on the floor coloring pictures. I had no idea he was paying attention to the tape explaining the closing technique of the alternative or subordinate question: "Do you want the red one or the blue one?" "Would you like the new car delivered next Tuesday or this Friday before the weekend?" Two days later as I was reading the morning paper, Ken came up to me and asked "Daddy, would you take me to Josh's house, or would you rather eat wood?" That phrase became a part of our household conversation for quite some time.

You can call it influence, pull, or anything you like. I call it leadership through dynamic responsiveness. There will always be a place in our world for people who are responsive to the needs of others, no matter how high-tech we become.

LEADERS HAVE A RESPONSIVE STATE OF MIND

I've always been fascinated by the sled dogs that once provided the primary transportation in northern Alaska and Canada, and now are used extensively for racing. It would be difficult to find a better example of teamwork and a better source of insights into how people can work together more effectively.

"Sled dogs love to race," writes Lorna Coppinger in *USAir* Magazine. "The dogs run in concert, sometimes even in step. To an observer the team may appear homogeneous, which at one level it is, but the driver knows he's guiding a team of individuals.

"The leader is fast, responsive to commands, and unafraid to be out in front of six, ten, or 14 dogs that will run right over him if he falters," she continues. "It's the lead dog that is so responsive to commands that you could write your name with your sled on a snow-covered lake. It's the leader that, footsore and spent, has such heart that he can bring an exhausted team in at a lope to finish a race with style."

It was interesting to me to note that each of the seven to fifteen dogs in a team has a position at which he runs best and contributes most to the race. In fact the drivers are so sensitive to each dog's performance that they often stop at various points of the race to shift the dogs' positions.

The dogs are so eager to run that race starters allow two minutes between dispatching each team to keep the dogs from getting tangled up in each other.

Can you imagine what you could do with a team of human huskies who were that enthusiastic, that responsive, and that committed to a common goal? Or can you imagine a crew of people so cooperative that they could be constantly shifted about so that each could fulfill a specific function at a given time?

What it boils down to is that each of the huskies sees himself as a leader in whatever role he's called upon to play. He is willing to both follow and give commands, and he is willing to give his best in doing either. But the dog that sets the pace always gains the coveted lead position.

That's what Dynamic Responsiveness is all about—seeking high achievement and seeking to inspire it in others in whatever position you find yourself. Dynamic Responsiveness is working as if the team's success rests upon your shoulders, but cooperating as if you can do nothing alone.

As president of a service company, with major corporations for clients, I find that one of the most challenging aspects of my job is that I constantly have to change hats. Sometimes I'm the chief executive giving direction and making vital decisions. At other times, I'm a coworker pitching in to help with the dirty work. At still other times, I'm a salesman pitching a new client or a troubleshooter solving a problem in one of our operations. In all those roles, I've found that the husky's attitude is my most valuable asset.

The husky's attitude is a state of mind that comes from a willingness to do whatever it takes to make sure the whole team reaches its goal. Life's responsive leaders see themselves as connected with the whole human race. They act like huskies in *all* their relationships, whether family, work, worship, or play.

In *Peak Performance Principles for High Achievers*, I listed six attitudes that are essential for becoming a high achiever. Interestingly, they are the same essential attitudes for leading others to high achievement.

1. High achievers are willing to make no small plans.
2. High achievers are willing to do what they fear.
3. High achievers are willing to prepare.
4. High achievers are willing to risk failure.
5. High achievers are teachable.
6. High achievers have heart.

LEADERS SET THE PACE

Lorna Coppinger points out that each husky in a dogsled team plays a vital role, "Yet in spite of the distinctiveness of each dog, it is the leader that represents the romance of the dog team. As stalwart and reliable as a wheel dog (one which runs at the back of the pack) might be, it is rare that a wheeler inspires the affection and lasting memory of 'the best dog I ever had' that drivers ascribe to that once-in-a-lifetime leader, always reliant for a fast, trouble-free race."

Why is the lead dog so important? In a grueling race, the leader is the one that must "animate the tiring team and bring it in at a good pace."

A responsive leader must do exactly the same thing for any human organization. He or she must set the pace for others to follow, inspire others to give their very best, and seek to bring out the best in every team member.

> No team ever finishes
> ahead of its leader.

It is accurate to say that no team ever finishes ahead of its leader. That's why leaders must be dynamically responsive to others. They can inspire the best in others only when they know what each team member can best contribute and know how to enable and inspire that person to give it.

ROLES OF A RESPONSIVE LEADER

While a husky's attitude is crucial, it's only the beginning of becoming a dynamic leader through responsiveness. Many people who are responsive never move to the front of the pack. The few who move to the front understand the roles a leader must play and master the basic skills of leadership.

First, let's turn our attention to the many vital roles a

95

leader must play, and how responsiveness can enable you to fulfill those roles in our increasingly high-tech world.

Role 1: A Responsive Leader Must Be Visionary

There are two dimensions to this vital function for the leader. The first dimension is the ability to see for yourself the potential of other people, to spot goals worthy of the group you would lead, and to believe you can enable that group to reach those goals. You must be able to look beyond petty prejudices and biases, beyond routine annoyances of daily living, and beyond discouraging circumstances.

A visionary teacher views students positively and tries to find and maximize their individual strengths. In this way, the teacher encourages cooperation and enthusiasm among the group. A nonvisionary teacher who tells students they are lazy or dumb creates a negative atmosphere conducive to rebellious behavior.

A responsive leader sees a solution for every problem rather than a problem for every solution, has ideas rather than excuses, and says, "We can!" when others say, "We can't!"

The second dimension is the ability to impart the vision to others. A responsive leader can make confidence live in the hearts of those who follow. So vital is this task of communicating your vision to others that we will devote a whole chapter to it later.

The difference
between a dream and a goal
is a plan.

96

Paul "Bear" Bryant, legendary coach of the University of Alabama, persuaded his teams to win games by communicating his vision in the simplest terms. When a sportscaster asked how he managed to consistently win more games than he lost, Bryant replied, "First, you've got to keep from gettin' beat; then you've got to beat the other team." "But how do you manage to do that?" asked the sportscaster. "Well," drawled Bryant, "you have to keep the other team from scoring more points than you do, and then you have to score more points than they do."

Role 2: A Responsive Leader Must Plan

Visions are only pipe dreams until someone comes up with concrete plans and strategies for making them reality. Responsive leaders are not satisfied to live with Murphy's Law, "If anything can go wrong, it will go wrong!" They develop a plan that will succeed no matter what goes wrong. The difference between a dream and a goal is a plan. A dream makes you feel good, but a goal makes you feel unrest and drives you into action.

Few people realize that when Neil Armstrong and Edwin Aldrin, Jr., landed their spacecraft on the moon's surface in 1969, it was the first time they had ever flown the lunar lander. How did they manage to accomplish this feat? They followed a plan that required them to practice in a simulator identical in every detail to the spacecraft. Then they applied the skills they learned on the ground to their space adventure.

A similar use of planning can facilitate the training of employees. When training materials and procedures are consistent with the actual equipment and work processes, employees can readily use what they learn. If they receive only training of a general nature, they will be much less successful. A lack of careful attention to the job and what it entails will almost certainly guarantee that the training will be incomplete.

Role 3: A Responsive Leader Must Guide Others Toward the Common Goal

An increasing number of outstanding athletes are "seeing themselves through to victory." Before a big event, they close their eyes and focus on a mental image of themselves reaching their goal.

If the leader has not previously achieved the goal to which he or she would lead others, it is absolutely essential that the leader envision the goal accomplished. Only then can the leader inspire others to reach it.

But a word of caution: A responsive leader knows that others must do things for themselves, yet a visionary person sometimes tends to jump in and take over when things seem to be dragging.

One of the toughest challenges I had to face in converting my company to professional management was to discipline myself to delegate tasks and allow people the freedom to manage those tasks through to completion. When I saw them faltering, making mistakes, or doing things differently from the way I would do them, the visionary within me wanted to jump in and take over. But I was so committed to the principles of Dynamic Responsiveness that I worked hard at being patient and allowing people the opportunity to develop. Now I'm really glad I did.

Admittedly, patience came hard to me. But what helped to ease the pressure I felt was realizing that I couldn't do everybody's job and still fulfill my roles as a leader.

Role 4: A Responsive Leader
Must Motivate Others Constantly

"How do you reward your salespeople when they reach their quotas?" someone asked the president of a large company.

"I let them keep their jobs!" came the quick response.

I was not surprised to discover the average tenure of his salespeople was slightly more than three years. It struck me as being an expensive way to do business, especially since selling the company's product required a moderately high level of skill.

The key to all motivation is desire, and the master key to creating desire is responsiveness to the needs, desires, and interests of the people you would lead.

A responsive leader knows that positive motivation will be communicated dramatically by open support of people. Sticking up for people when they are criticized for something they did not do, giving credit where it is due, or acknowledging individuals for their consistently good performance conveys a clear, meaningful message.

Role 5: A Responsive Leader
Coordinates All Resources

Much like the driver of a dogsled, the responsive leader chooses people who can get the job done, fits them into the slots where they can contribute most, trains and equips them to do their tasks well, and creates a climate in which they can all work together for maximum output.

It is never enough to make sure everybody is working hard. The responsive leader must constantly strive to maintain a climate in which every member of the team can learn, develop, and achieve at a very high level.

Before the housekeeping training instructors on our staff

begin a session with a client's employees, they coordinate their resources. They assemble the correct equipment and make sure it's in top condition. They organize the training materials and aids. And they hold the session in a location as close to the normal work environment as possible.

Then they go a step further. They put the attendees at ease by explaining the reason for the training and by discussing the importance of the attendees' job. The instructors encourage questions so that they can find out what the individuals already know and what they need to know. After that, the training begins.

Role 6: A Responsive Leader
Is a Troubleshooter

Responsive leaders are concerned with fixing the problem instead of fixing the blame. Taking a positive view of any mishap or delay, the responsive leader asks questions like, "Where do we go from here?" or "How can we get it working again?"

Marilyn had been on her new job as an office manager less than a week when it became apparent that she was facing a productivity problem in her section. Instead of wasting time blaming her predecessor for the situation (which would have solved nothing), she pinpointed the cause of the problem by talking with employees, reviewing their workloads, and evaluating the work flow in general. By taking a positive view, she found that low productivity was a direct result of unclear priorities. Major assignments were being delayed to the last minute, while routine tasks were being tackled immediately "to get them out of the way." Marilyn, in consultation with the employees involved, established a priority-ranking system along with a flexible schedule that enabled large jobs to be taken care of as "routinely" as the small jobs. Office productivity increased, and the employees were pleased with their performance—and with their new manager.

Role 7: A Responsive Leader Is a Cheerleader

Responsive leaders know that praise and compliments are the oil that make human machinery run smoothly. Instead of concerning themselves with being recognized, they concern themselves with recognizing others. For them, it is enough to achieve high goals. It is amazing what you can accomplish when you don't care who gets the credit.

> It is amazing what you can accomplish
> when you don't care who gets the credit.

An advertising agency had experienced chronic difficulty in getting promotional catalogs designed and produced on time, and a major client was threatening to withdraw its account. Steve, the new account executive, knew that this one client could make or break his ties with the agency. Steve confidently assured the client that the agency's most talented creative director, Jim, personally would oversee the catalog's design and production. Jim had been in charge of the catalog all along but had not been given the authority to make it happen, and nobody in the agency had ever acknowledged his vital role to the client. So far as the client knew, the catalog had always been designed and produced by "staff." Pleased that he was being credited for his work, Jim was especially attentive to the job at hand—a well-designed catalog produced on time. His finished design was especially innovative and creative, and the finished product was ready two days before the deadline. The client loved it. Jim was pleased with the recognition and praise he received from the client, and Steve was pleased that he had met the agency's goals. Steve was a cheerleader for a player who had learned the thrill of winning.

Everyone has the need to be appreciated. Your genuinely honest expression of appreciation can really motivate people, and you may be surprised that your own self-confidence is boosted. By being complimentary instead of critical, you create a climate in which people are more willing to reciprocate with compliments. As a result, your work, family, and life will be more pleasant.

TYING IT ALL TOGETHER

Dynamic Responsiveness begins as a state of mind that can best be described as a husky's attitude. From there it moves to fulfilling the leadership roles with enthusiasm and expertise. And that leads us to the skills of Dynamic Responsiveness, the subject of our second section.

SECTION TWO

How to Master the Skills of Dynamic Responsiveness

My greatest expert guide of all time is Jesus. None of the world's great leaders has ever had so much impact on contemporaries and succeeding generations. He was also the most brilliant organizer and executive the world has ever known.

In Chapter Three, we saw that one of the things that made Jesus so effective as a leader was that He was always responsive to the people around him.

His challenge for us to love others as He has loved us compels us to look further at the skills which express that responsiveness. Because this book is meant to be practical, it makes sense to explore the skills and methods of responsive people.

Space will allow us to devote only a short chapter to each of the more outstanding skills. And, since our thrust is developing people power, we will devote most of our space to how to develop and use those skills to become a powerful and responsive leader in the electronic age.

Together, we will explore:

1. How to listen responsively.
2. How to communicate responsively.
3. How to set goals for high achievement.
4. How to plan for responsive action.
5. How to choose and channel people for high achievement.
6. How to equip people for high achievement.
7. How to hold responsive meetings.
8. How to be a tiger, not a pussycat.

We also will explore how each of those skills fits into the Dynamic Responsiveness System of relating to people and how you can become a responsive person.

SIX

How to Listen Responsively

They call it "the ultimate listening device." Looking like a gigantic radar antenna, it sits atop a bleak, ice-covered hill near the North Pole. Twenty-four hours each day, 365 days each year, it sends out signals that travel deep into outer space—farther than any messages have ever gone. The mission? To see if anybody is out there listening. Out the signals go, while scientists wait quietly for any response.

In a way, this sort of activity is a symbol for our high-tech mind-set. As scientists clamor to be heard by intelligent life which may or may not exist galaxies away, millions of people cry out to be heard by someone close enough to touch.

- A father fails to hear a child's bid for attention because there is no time.
- A couple exchange blank stares because they no longer speak the same language.
- An executive ignores an idea worth millions because thousands are at stake in the stock market.
- A woman orders a hamburger and gets a fish sandwich because a clerk is preoccupied.
- A man jogging for his health gets killed by a screaming ambulance because his mini-stereo is too loud.

Despite the fact that more sophisticated listening devices are available now than ever before, many communications experts believe fewer and fewer communications are getting through. In this chapter we will discuss (1) what is listening; (2) what is *responsive* listening; (3) how responsive listening can make you dynamic; (4) why responsive listening is so powerful; (5) how responsively do you listen; and (6) how you can become a better listener.

WHAT IS LISTENING?

The single most crucial skill of the Dynamic Responsiveness System is listening. Does that mean that if you have good ears you are a good listener? Certainly not!

Helen Keller was one of the best listeners the world has ever known, yet she could not hear the loudest yell. Author, philanthropist, and an inspiration to all who knew her, she achieved international fame without the capacity to hear, see, or speak.

Hearing is merely the physical faculty for sensing and deciphering sounds. As sensitive as the human ears are, they are no match for those of a cat or a deer or a wolf. If hearing were all that was involved, many of the lower animals would greatly outdistance human beings as listeners.

But listening suggests more than merely hearing. It suggests what my friend and colleague Nido Qubein calls "the high art of paying attention." Listening involves the full capacity of your mind, body, and spirit not only to receive the messages sent but also to discern the meanings behind them.

BUT WHAT DO WE MEAN BY RESPONSIVE LISTENING?

In a sense, all listening is responsive, but as we use the term, responsive listening goes one step further. Responsive listening seeks to receive and affirm the person behind the messages and meanings.

> Responsive listening can present a *threat*
> to the insecure because it involves
> laying aside prejudices and biases.

Responsive listening is active, alert, vigilant, sensitive, and creative. It means paying attention with the goal of responding positively to the person. It means utilizing all your faculties—ears, eyes, brain, emotions, spirit, and sometimes even touch—to become aware of another's needs, interests, and concerns.

Responsive listening takes *time* because it calls for more than merely grabbing a few choice words and translating them to fit preconceived meanings. Responsive listening takes *energy* because it requires more than keeping one ear open and one track of your brain working. Responsive listening can present a *threat* to the insecure because it involves laying aside prejudices and biases.

But, interestingly, responsive listening can save you much more than it costs because it can keep you from losing valuable resources, help you reduce costly mistakes, prevent having to do things over, and be a means for mustering support to reach your goals.

HOW RESPONSIVE LISTENING
CAN MAKE YOU DYNAMIC

What does responsive listening have to do with the Dynamic Responsiveness System? Much, in every way. Let's see how it fits with the four components of the system.

1. *Value people (including yourself) above everything but God.* The most loving thing you can do for people is to listen responsively to them. It expresses interest, indicates concern, and shows that you care.

It's not unusual for a skilled counselor to sit for an hour, not saying much but listening responsively, while a troubled person unloads all his or her mental anguish. When the session ends, the person will say, "You'll never know how much you've helped me!" "All I did was listen!" the counselor may protest. But it was enough.

How does responsive listening fit with valuing yourself? Absolutely nothing can win affection, loyalty, and support for your goals as effectively as responsive listening. On the one hand it is the most unselfish thing you can do, but on the other hand it is the most self-rewarding thing you can do.

2. *Give to people what you want to get from people.* One of the most overpowering needs we all have is the need to be understood. Perhaps that's why we should go to such great lengths to explain our motivations and actions to those we really care about.

Since the greatest aid to understanding people is responsive listening, we can give nothing greater. Responsive listening is love in action. Nowhere is it more appropriate than within the family. If it's not done there, it's probably not being done on the job either.

When someone says, "Nobody understands me," what is really meant is, "Nobody listens to me." There is no better way to understand your spouse, your children, your friends, or your coworkers than to give them some time to talk to you. When people recognize your willingness to listen and learn about them, they will be more willing to listen to you.

3. *Make cooperation a way of life.* A simple invitation like "Tell me how you feel about that" or "Tell me what you think" can be one of the greatest ways available to show a cooperative attitude. By doing this, you are telling the person, "You matter to me, so I want to cooperate with you." And if you take seriously what you hear after you've extended that invitation, you'll be amazed at how much cooperation it can win for you.

Ninety-nine times out of one hundred, an industrial relations supervisor will tell an employee what is going to be done for him or to him. Many customer service departments (and parents) handle complaints the same way. But I don't think you can win anyone's cooperation using that method. Instead, ask what the individual would like you to do about the situation, and your willingness to listen and cooperate usually will be reciprocated.

4. *Keep doing it!* Responsive listening must be persistent. It must push through until interests, needs, and concerns are expressed.

Over fifty years ago, Edwin Markham wrote a poem about a man who drew a circle around himself to shut others out. But love and the poet won him over—"We drew a circle that took him in!" When someone draws a tiny circle around himself, responsive listening keeps drawing larger circles to take him in.

You simply cannot be a responsive leader without being a responsive listener. And the better you become at it, the more valuable and dynamic you become.

WHY RESPONSIVE LISTENING IS SO POWERFUL

A major problem of living in a high-tech world is that we are barraged with so many signals from so many sources that we simply cannot absorb them all. To defend ourselves against sensory overload, we become masters at tuning out unwanted signals. This is such a reflexive, automatic reaction that most of us are not aware we do it.

We listen with one ear (if that's possible), reach a quick conclusion about what the other person is saying, and turn our attention to something else when a friend or loved one wants to pour out his or her heart to us.

Our all-too-common practice of insincere greeting rituals illustrates our real reluctance to listen responsively. Let's see how this works. Bob sees James, his down-the-street neighbor, coming out of the bank one afternoon. Bob says, "Hi! How are you?" Expecting the usual I'm-doing-fine response, Bob is surprised and then somewhat disconcerted when James begins to tell how he really is. The more James talks, the more uncomfortable Bob becomes, and instead of listening to his neighbor in need, he tries to figure out a way to escape the situation as soon as possible.

The recipient of such half-hearted listening interprets it as rejection. Perhaps that explains why sometimes individuals approach strangers in a supermarket or airport and begin telling the deepest concerns of their lives. People search desperately for someone to care enough to listen responsively to them.

If you've ever tried responsive listening, you know that it is powerful stuff. But have you thought about why? Perhaps you've never really thought about how valuable responsive listening can make you to other people and what leverage it can give you in leading others to high achievement. Let's focus on some of the many results of responsive listening.

Result 1: You Break Down Barriers

We erect emotional barriers to protect ourselves from those we believe will hurt us. Even people who seem aggressive or overly assertive are hiding behind barriers because they are afraid of others. Responsive listening is an effective way to say, "I won't hurt you! Let's negotiate!" Defensiveness from others goes down in inverse proportion to the degree you listen responsively. The more responsive you are, the less defensive they are. And the more open people are to you, the easier it becomes to get your messages through and to lead them in the direction you want them to go.

> Defensiveness from others goes down
> in inverse proportion to the degree
> you listen responsively.

A wise manager once gave me sound advice about how to break down defenses. He said, "Just ask why and keep on asking why." If a person is pressing you or avoiding you, try to open up the discussion by asking "why" questions. Make the other person prove his point, follow his questions with your questions and lead him into the real area of disagreement. You must break through the defenses before workable solutions can be found.

Result 2: You Express Interest and Concern

The opposite of love is not hate, it's apathy. You cannot ignore a person and listen responsively at the same time. The responsive listener says, "I value you as a human being and treasure your ideas, needs, and concerns."

One caution: You can't fake it. People can sense a phony,

half-hearted listener. Pretending to care, when you'd really rather be doing something else, makes you come across as condescending. And nobody likes to be patronized. You can only get positive results from responsive listening when you really care about people.

Betty spotted Joan, a member of her service organization, while she was shopping at the mall one evening and immediately bustled over to her. "Joan, dear, I understand that your son has been quite ill. How is he now?" As Joan started to tell her, Betty tried to catch the eye of a sales clerk while she made listening "noises" in response to Joan, "Uh-huh. Is that right? Oh, that's too bad." Joan quickly got the message and excused herself, resolving not to discuss her personal life with Betty again.

Result 3: You Gain Valuable Insights

Responsive listening is like an open window through which you can see into another person's motivations, needs, desires, and interests. If it's true that the greatest way to succeed in business is to find a need and fill it, responsive listening can make you very successful in your business as well as your personal life.

Remember, people will give their very best—even lay their lives on the line—for a person they believe really understands their needs and genuinely responds to them.

When I first started in the industrial cleaning business, I almost blew it trying to sell services to my first nationally known client, the Indianapolis Motor Speedway, an institution I'd held in awe since my childhood. When Clarence Cagle, the renowned expert on track surfaces who was in charge of maintenance and facilities, agreed to see me, I rushed to the track. I got there an hour before my appointment so I could thoroughly study his needs before I met with him. I was loaded with ideas of how we could serve him, and when his secretary showed me into his office, I must have sounded like a race car whose driver had just seen the green light.

First, I offered to bring our heavy-duty equipment out each night during the time trials and clean up the tire marks left by cars that spin out, the flash fire marks left by magnesium wheels when they hit the white walls of the track, and the oil and tire residue that builds up in the grooves through the turns. Slowly he shook his head and told me the United States Auto Club (USAC) and the speedway could be sued right out of business if he let me so much as touch that track with chemical applications or pressure washing. Strike one.

Next, I told him how we could clean up all the oil and grease on the floors in the garages where the mechanics work on the cars. "Young man," he said indignantly, "those garages are immaculate. The minute a drop of oil hits the floor, a mechanic is there with a rag to wipe it up." Strike two.

Finally, I decided to quit talking and listen responsively. "Do you have any cleaning problems?" I asked rather humbly. Suddenly his interest in our conversation picked up. He rose to his feet, motioned for me to follow him outside, and showed me thousands of metal folding chairs. "That's my biggest cleaning problem—cleaning all those chairs," he announced. "If you could figure out a better way to do it, you'd have a job out here every year," he added quickly. Responsive listening paid off. I had myself a sale and a long-term relationship with a client which gave our business instant credibility as legitimate and capable.

That one sale made executives from some of the biggest industries in our area sit up and take notice, and it helped immeasurably to boost us into a multi-million-dollar cleaning-management service having served more than two hundred clients in several states.

113

What made the difference? I discovered a need I could fill when I quit talking and started listening responsively.

Result 4: You Encourage Communication

Do you know what a *monologue in duet* is? That's where you think up what you're going to say while the other person says what he thought up while you were talking. Unfortunately, too many of our interchanges are monologues in duet.

> I discovered a need I could fill
> when I quit talking and started listening
> responsively.

Don't you just hate it when your phone rings in the middle of a nice nap, and you answer it, only to find you're listening to some spiel about lifetime light bulbs or a prize you've just been selected to compete for? You stand there and nod and wait for a break in the monologue. When the break finally comes, you feel like telling the machine gun voice that you don't have electricity or that you own the company that manufactures the prize they're giving away.

What makes that sort of phone call so unpleasant is that we are totally uninvolved in the conversation. It's as if our needs, interests, and desires don't count. (Perhaps that explains why such telephone solicitations produce only about 3 to 5 percent positive response.)

Whether you're selling light bulbs, trying to win the affection of a family member, or trying to talk a meter maid out of a parking ticket, you won't make much progress until the other person is involved in the process. The best way to do that is through responsive listening.

Result 5: You Clear Up Misconceptions

How many mistakes could be avoided, how much money could be saved, how many heartaches could be prevented, if we would just learn how to listen responsively?

Communication involves more than words. It involves meanings. If I say, "He is cool," am I suggesting someone turn up the thermostat? Or maybe that the fever has broken? Or that he is distant? Or that he can handle pressure? Perhaps he's suave? Could it be he's arty or knows his jazz? Maybe he's up on the latest fashion? I could even give a sigh of relief because the air conditioner has been fixed and the boss is finally comfortable.

Words are our most effective tools for conveying meanings, yet they are imprecise, often have varied meanings, can be changed by usage, and are often misused. To add to the confusion, words change from one locale or time to another.

Only when we cut through the fog surrounding communication attempts can we zero in on specific meanings. The best way to do this is to listen responsively.

Result 6: You Learn

A friend of mine once remarked that he had learned what it means to be loved without reservation. When asked how, he replied, "I've spent the weekend working in a camp for retarded children. They don't question; they just reach out with total abandon."

I like the way Ralph Waldo Emerson expressed it, "Every

> It is by questioning what we think
> that we can come to know.

man I meet is in some way my superior, and, in that, I can learn of him."

Interestingly, one of the most valuable things we can learn is how to phrase the proper questions to get the answers we want. Only the bigot refuses to submit his or her opinions to the questionings of others. It is by questioning what we think that we can come to know.

Shopping at the Straw Market in Saint Martin, my wife and I met two little boys who knew all about the value of phrasing questions. "Hey, mister, bet'cha I can tell you where you got 'em shoes," challenged the smaller of the two.

"No, thanks," I replied.

"Come on, mister," he persisted. "Bet'cha I can tell you where you got 'em shoes."

"I'm not interested," I replied as I steered my wife through the maze of goods.

"What's the matter? Ain't you got a buck to bet?"

I could see it was not going to be easy to escape so I relented, "All right. Where do you think I got these shoes?"

He grinned up at me and said, "You got 'em shoes on the sidewalk outside the Straw Market in Saint Martin. Give me my buck."

Here, we only have space to list a few of the many exciting benefits to be gained from responsive listening. However, even a casual reading of these should convince you that responsive listening is one of the most valuable aids to communicating, showing you care, and learning how to relate more effectively with other people.

HOW RESPONSIVELY DO YOU LISTEN?

Perhaps you think you are already a responsive listener. If you are, chances are pretty good that you will enjoy learning how to do it even better. But before you rate yourself as a good listener, take a look at the following ways you can tell just how good you are.

You know you're a responsive listener when . . .

1. You'd rather listen than talk.
2. Others comment that you're easy to talk to because you encourage them to talk.
3. You listen openly to all people regardless of their status, gender, or race.
4. You gladly put away whatever you are doing while someone else is talking.
5. You find it easy to look the speaker straight in the eyes.
6. You find it easy to ignore distractions while you're listening to someone talk.
7. You get your whole body involved; you smile, nod your head, make gestures, and so forth.
8. You don't allow yourself to think faster than the person is talking, but concentrate totally on what is being said.
9. You search for the meanings behind the words by asking questions, by restating what you think you've heard, and by watching the person's expressions.
10. You gladly avoid interrupting, but graciously yield to being interrupted.
11. You keep probing when there is any doubt about what the person means.
12. You listen equally well to a compliment or a complaint, regardless of the tone of voice.
13. You listen fully to the person's explanation before you form an opinion about his or her ideas.
14. You make notes, especially when the person talks fast.
15. You find it easy to say, "Tell me more."

16. You readily identify with the person's feelings and motives, and you're sympathetic even if you disagree.
17. You readily acknowledge that what seems trivial to you may seem vital to the talker.
18. You willingly change your opinions when given valid reasons.
19. You don't squelch the freedom of choice of others but willingly help them express what they feel, explore their options, and suggest new ideas they might consider.
20. People cooperate readily with you because they feel you value them, respect their opinions (even if you disagree), and understand their motives.

Wow! Wouldn't it be great if every person we encountered each day were that kind of listener? I don't like to make bets, but the odds are so great that I'd almost violate that rule and bet that if we lived in a world full of listeners like that, we could eliminate our nuclear arms, wipe out all traces of hunger, and quickly conquer our most dreaded diseases. Relating to people would be a breeze.

Of course, none of us can promise that every person we meet will listen like that, but all of us can promise that every person we meet will find us increasingly willing to listen like that. It's a way of giving others what we'd like to receive.

HOW YOU CAN BECOME A BETTER LISTENER

Responsive listening is a skill and, as all skills, can be improved by learning more about it and practicing it more often. Make a copy of the following pointers and put them where you can review them often in order to practice them regularly. I promise that the more you practice them, and the better you become at using them, the more effective you'll become at working with people in every area of life.

Pointer 1: Slow Down

Haste is the greatest barrier to responsive listening. You'll be amazed at how much time you can save by listening carefully, because
   A. You'll have less to do over.
   B. People will be more willing to help you.
   C. You'll be sure people understand you more correctly.
   D. You can diagnose problems and discover solutions more quickly.

Pointer 2: Take Care of Your Listening Time

Allocate your listening by priorities. Don't be hesitant to say warmly, "I really want to hear what you have to say. Let's set up a time when I can give you my full attention."

Pointer 3: Concentrate Fully on What's Being Said

Push aside all papers except your notepad, clear your mind of all preoccupations, lay aside all biases, start listening with the first sentence, and don't stop listening until the person has finished.

Pointer 4: Grant a Fair Hearing

Granting a fair hearing means
   A. Never interrupting.
   B. Withholding all judgments until the person finishes.

C. Looking for meanings and feelings behind the words.
D. Being tactful but honest and direct.
E. Not letting the person's ability (or lack of ability) to express things get in your way. Focus on what is being said, not on how it is being said.

Pointer 5: Make It Easy for the Person to Talk

In order to make it easy for a person to talk,
A. Push aside all interruptions and distractions. (Nothing makes it harder for a person to talk than having to pause while you take phone calls or talk to other people.)
B. Ask questions to stimulate conversation.
C. Use facial expressions, gestures, and body language to encourage the person to talk.

Pointer 6: Make Sure You Understand Completely

If you're not sure about a point,
A. Ask questions to clarify it.
B. Restate what you understand to make sure you have understood what the person meant.
C. Make notes of important points.
D. Avoid jumping to conclusions.

Pointer 7: Clarify Expectations

Make sure both you and the talker understand what actions are to be taken after the interchange is over. A brief review can do wonders to correct misconceptions and eliminate false expectations.

TYING IT ALL TOGETHER

Responsive listening can do more to make you a dynamic person than any other skill you can master. It is the most effective way to

- Show you value people.
- Give what you want most to receive from others.
- Make cooperation a way of life.
- Keep doing it . . . until you understand and win people over.

It's the best way to receive messages.

C H A P T E R

SEVEN

How to Communicate Responsively

Computer specialists like to throw around the term *GIGO*, an acronym that means "garbage in = garbage out." And with computers it's that simple.

Even the most sophisticated computers do only one thing: They store data. Computers are completely passive. They have no feelings, no opinions, no thoughts or ideas, no interests, and their only need is for electricity. They gobble up each byte of information and keep it unchanged as long as the current is sufficient to hold it.

Everything else in data processing depends upon the software, equipment, programs, and users. Data fed into the computer are stored accurately and without question, without regard to how new data relate to other data previously received. Computers have no desire, need, or interest in doing anything with the data.

Anyone, therefore, who compares programming a computer to communicating with human beings shows little understanding of either. You can learn how to program a simple computer in a matter of days, a more complex system in a matter of weeks, and even the most complex systems within a few months or years. But you can spend a lifetime learning how to communicate with human beings.

WHY IT IS SO HARD
TO COMMUNICATE EFFECTIVELY

"I've told you a thousand times, and you still haven't heard me!" shouts a distraught mother to a teenaged son, or a frustrated manager to an employee, or a disgruntled customer to an unresponsive clerk.

Sadly, that person might try a thousand more times without much more success. Perhaps even more sadly, the person may simply give up and quit trying.

At the very best, communicating with human beings is a complex and imperfect art. In fact, most people don't realize how complex it is. They may assume that they are better communicators than they are, that when communication fails it is because the other person just didn't listen, or that others will figure out what they want anyway.

FACTORS THAT COMPLICATE COMMUNICATION

First, let's look at why communicating is so complex, then we'll turn our attention to how we can do it more effectively.

Factor 1: People Are on the Run

Everybody seems to be in such a hurry these days. "Just give it to me straight. I don't have time for explanations," is a fairly common response.

We find ourselves having to give a simple yes or no answer to complex questions. In business, the big question is, "What's the bottom line?" There's no time to consider variables or possibilities—just results.

The dangers of miscommunication increase with the speed at which messages must be sent and received. And

123

unfortunately, the "bottom line" is that things are going to get worse. As the workweek shortens, the pace quickens, and people find more to do with their time, communicating with others will become increasingly rushed.

Factor 2: So Many Voices Are Competing

On the average, the typical person receives about 1,500 messages per day, ranging from simple greetings and media commercials to complex instructions. Our attempts to communicate must compete with all the other voices crying for attention.

> The dangers of miscommunications
> increase with the speed at which messages
> must be sent and received.

Your letter requesting a job interview, for example, will probably fall onto the desk of an executive at the same time he or she receives a stack of junk mail.

Factor 3: Messages Vital to Us May Be of Only Passing Interest to Others

A minister who spends a whole week preparing a sermon must deliver it to a congregation of people who are preoccupied with roasts in the oven, afternoon football games, or next week's agenda.

We have to compete for attention with all the events and emotions running through the minds of our audiences. A waitress who's depressed over a lost love, a secretary who's worried about a sick child, or an executive who's concerned with investments gone sour might find it hard to listen with interest to our simple request.

Factor 4: Few People Are Good Listeners

We make a big deal out of it when a baby says the first word, when children are taught how to speak and write, and when the mass media hire specialists at saying things. Yet our society seems to put little emphasis on the crucial task of listening.

Occasionally a TV situation comedy will include a segment that shows how little listening is done even within the family. The scene might go something like this: George is reading the evening paper, and Mary is trying to discuss a problem their child is having in school. After a few sentences, she realizes George isn't listening to her, and she makes a few outlandish statements to try to get his attention. Usually the scene ends with Mary saying something like, "Well, I think I'll just go pack a few things, drive to the airport, and catch a plane to Paris so I can begin my new life as an artist," and George answers, "That's nice, dear." We may laugh, but it's not that amusing in real-life situations.

We simply must face the fact that, on average, less than 20 percent of what we say will be heard, understood, and acted upon.

Less than 20 percent
of what we say
will be heard, understood,
and acted upon.

Factor 5: Communicating Is an Imprecise Art

Few people are able to express precisely what they want to say. And even the best communicators occasionally send out confusing messages. If you are of average intelligence, or even slightly above average, you can count on nearly half your messages being less than clear. For example, expressions such as "you know" or "you know what I mean" are fairly common to people who send out confusing messages. How can anyone know what they mean if they can't be more precise?

One reason for this is that words in themselves are confusing. The 500 most commonly used words in the English language have more than 14,000 meanings—an average of 28 meanings per word. When you add the more than 700,000 types of nonverbal messages we send along with those words, it's not hard to see how complex it is to send a simple message that can be easily understood by a variety of people.

For example, I heard recently about a schoolteacher who wanted to order 144 pencils. She wrote out her order, *144 pencils—gross*. Simple enough, right? Wrong! A few weeks later she received 20,736 pencils—144 gross—and a bill for more than $4,000.

The point of all this is not to convince you it is impossible to communicate effectively. For all its hazards, most of us still find ways to communicate with those people who really matter to us. Each year, millions of couples get married, millions of people find jobs, and somehow, billions of pencils get sold at a profit.

It matters not how poor you are now at communicating, you can learn to become an effective communicator. Likewise, no matter how good you are at it now, you can always become more effective.

The starting point is to understand the difficulties you face in communicating with the people you see every day. Once you understand some of the difficulties, you will be able to see the value in each of the methods we will explore together.

ALL EFFECTIVE COMMUNICATION IS RESPONSIVE

Responsive communication is not new. In a simpler era, an aircraft mechanic would position himself to spin the propeller of a biplane and yell "Contact." The pilot would check the magneto, the throttle, and the fuel mixture control; then yell back "CONTACT!" The stakes were not so high, but the system worked.

Back then they called it dialogue, which simply meant two people talking *with* each other, exchanging meanings, acknowledging each other, and adjusting their understandings. Dialogue involved the audience as an active participant in the communication process.

As the mass media flourished, however, audience participation became passive, and responses were tallied up in surveys as yeses or noes.

But recently, a decided shift back to responsive communication, or dialogue, has occurred. Major corporations are now holding seminars for all their people to deal with such subjects as listening, writing effective memos, and improving intraoffice communication. It's as if thousands of executives have suddenly awakened to the sound of one hand clapping.

Salespeople are now being trained to try several trial closes during their presentations instead of merely giving a pitch, then asking for an order. Trainers are beginning to use teach-back techniques to determine how well they are doing their job by testing how much of what they've taught has been learned. And family therapists are using more and more structured listening exercises to help family members understand each other.

The point is that in our mad dash into the electronic age we lost much of the intimacy and responsiveness that give communication its vitality and effectiveness. Wise communicators are now seeking to rediscover the art of dialogue.

COMPUTERS JUST DON'T UNDERSTAND

James J. Kilpatrick, one of America's most celebrated writers, shared in his column* how he had recently bought a computer program to scan his copy for errors in spelling.

"I got more than I bargained for," he reported. "This piece of software not only flags errors in spelling, it also criticizes errors in 'grammar, usage, style and punctuation.'

"Out of curiosity," he continued, "I subjected some of my own sparkling prose to the ministrations of this floppy disk. The machine said I was a lousy writer.

"Then I fed the RightWriter Lincoln's Gettysburg Address. Abe was lousy too. This is what the computer said about old Abe: 'Readers need an 11th grade level education to understand the writing. The writing style is very weak. The writing is wordy. Passive voice is being heavily used. Many adjectives are being used. Most sentences contain multiple clauses. Try to use more simple sentences.'"

Poor old computer! How could it be expected to understand how an audience of grieving widows and parents felt? How could it understand patriotism? Or bravery? Or hopes for ending wars? Or freedom? Or slavery?

How can a system, which only stores and processes data, ever comprehend the emotions and values that could cause men to make slaves of their brothers, to risk life and limb to free people they'd never seen, or to struggle to pull together a divided nation?

But the people who heard that speech understood and cared. They cared, they hurt, they felt empty and lonely. They were moved to tears, hopes, and actions by the "wordy" speech. What's more, English teachers consider the Gettysburg Address a classic composition, and a hundred and twenty-five years later it's still being memorized by fifth-grade students all over this "one nation, under God, indivisible, with liberty and justice for all."

You simply cannot communicate with a machine—no matter how high-tech it may be—because communication has to do with meanings, with feelings, with ideas, with desires. Communication takes place between human beings because only humans can think, reason, understand, care, and attach meanings to symbols and images.

Those who communicate best rely upon responsiveness to touch the lives of others, to make their meanings understood, and to produce the results they desire.

UNDERSTANDING THE PROCESS

What do we mean when we say, "Communicate responsively"?

The word *communicate* comes from an ancient Greek word meaning "to make common." Later usage gave it the meaning "to cause to understand." And the root word for responsive is *respond*, which means "to answer." It comes from an old French word from which we get our term *spouse*. Literally, it means to "answer with a promise."

Okay, now that we have the technical definitions of the

> The primary goal of
> all responsive communication
> is to obtain
> a desired response.

words, what do they mean to us as we seek to work with and relate to people in the dailiness of life?

The primary goal of all responsive communication is to obtain a desired response. Let me illustrate: If a man asks a woman to marry him, he wants her to say yes. If a woman offers a product or service to a prospect, she wants that prospect to say, "I'll buy it." If you apply for a job, you want the prospective employer to offer you a job. If you ask someone to help you, you want help.

All this assumes, of course, that (1) you value the people you wish to communicate with; (2) you are willing to give what you want to get from others; (3) you have made cooperation a way of life; and (4) you are willing to keep sending and receiving messages until you achieve your desired goal—the cooperation of others.

It makes no difference whether you are trying to reach an audience of one person or thousands, responsive communication is an ongoing process of repeating four basic steps.

1. Gain and hold attention.
2. Convey your message accurately and adequately.
3. Gain the desired response.
4. Monitor your results.

Let's look closely at each one, and try to gain some insights as to how to do all of them.

> No worthwhile communication can take place
> until you have the attention of your audience.

Step 1: Gain and Hold Attention

All worthwhile communication is two-way communication.

- *Poor* communicators send messages, but don't concern themselves with response.
- *Average* communicators send messages, then look for response.
- *Responsive* communicators seek response before, during, and after sending their messages.

No worthwhile communication can take place until you have the attention of your audience. Whether you're talking to your mate, holding a staff meeting, or giving a major address to a huge audience, your first task is to gain the attention of your audience. And if that attention is ever lost, you must somehow regain it before you attempt to continue sending your messages. Ignoring that rule is like shouting, "I love you," to the ocean.

But how do you gain attention and hold it? How can you be sure a busy executive will pay attention to your letter amidst all the letters in the pile? How can you get a teenager to take off the headphones and listen to what you have to say? How can you be sure that your audience will sit up and take notice of what you have to say?

Here are some tips from some of America's most effective

communicators—professional public speakers. The tips center on speaking before an audience, but they can easily apply to all forms of communication.

Tip 1: Study Your Audience

What interests them? What do they want? What do they fear? How do they perceive their needs? What are the most compelling issues in their lives at that moment? What do they resist? The more questions you search out and answer, the better equipped you are to gain the audience's attention.

People who make television commercials know this tactic and use it well. With millions of dollars riding on every commercial, they want to make sure they grab the audience's attention from the first second. If they're trying to gain the attention of parents, they may show an adorable child doing something amusing in the opening scene. If their target audience is people who like high-performance cars, they might open with a car streaking through a sharp turn. When TV advertisers find a winner, they stick with it as long as it generates sales.

Do commercials work? There are two ways you can always tell if an advertising technique is working for its sponsors. First, the ad will be repeated over and over. How many times did you see a little old lady ask, "Where's the beef?" (And, by the same token, when was the last time you saw this commercial?) Second, if the technique works, it will be copied by other advertisers. How many beer commercials, for instance, are built around the theme of camaraderie for young, lonely singles?

The better you understand your audience, the better you can speak to their needs, interests, and concerns. And the better you do that, the better you can gain and hold attention.

Tip 2: Identify with Your Audience

What are the members of your audience feeling at the moment they receive your message? What motivates them? What would they like most to hear you say? Why would they listen to you? Why would they not listen to you? What would they least like to hear you say?

Obviously, you can't always say what people want to hear, but the more you understand about their preferences and attitudes, the more effectively you can bid for their attention.

For example, the people who create sweepstake offers understand and widely use this principle. I'm sure you get letters quite often that start out with your name in big bold letters, with the announcement, "Your name has been selected. . . ." As you read a little further, you discover that millions of other names have also "been selected," but the advertisers have achieved their goal of gaining your attention.

When you communicate responsively, you identify with your audience and make your bid for attention in the form of a response to what they are feeling. And it's always a good idea to use people's names in bidding for attention because most of us like to hear our names called.

Tip 3: Be Sensitive to Your Audience

What's going on with your audience at the moment of your bid for attention? Are they tired? Uncomfortable? Too comfortable? In a lousy mood?

A famous speaker was once introduced after his audience had been subjected to hours of announcements, recognitions, introductions, awards, and other speeches. His audience was clearly exhausted when he stood to speak.

"My message to you tonight is hope," he announced, "and right now, I know that your greatest hope is that I should finish quickly. So I shall. Thank you and good night!" With that, he sat down. But the audience rose to give him a standing ovation. Sometimes, the most productive thing you can say is nothing.

Dale Carnegie once called Frank Bettger the greatest salesman he'd ever known. One thing that made Bettger so effective was that he was always sensitive to his audience. His practice was to ask for five minutes of their time and to promise to stay longer only if they asked him to do so. Always, when his five minutes were up, he'd stand to his feet and announce that he'd used up his time and was leaving. Almost invariably, he was invited to stay longer.

> The person who has been heard and understood
> is usually more willing to listen and understand.

Tip 4: Pay Attention to Your Audience

The best way to get your audience to pay attention to you is to pay attention to them. Nothing opens the door for you to convey your message more effectively than listening to the other person. The person who has been heard and understood is usually more willing to listen and understand. It's another way of giving what you want to get from others.

Try this approach sometime when you are being raked over the coals by an irate person:

1. Listen without interrupting while the person vents his or her rage.
2. Show you understand with a comment like, "I wouldn't like to be treated that way, either." Then wait while the person lets it all out.

3. Ask, "What would you like for me to do to make it right?" Very often the person will say, "Oh, it's no big deal. I just wanted to let you know I didn't like it." Even if some unreasonable demands are made, you have defused his or her anger enough that you can reason together and come to some mutually satisfying agreement.

Tip 5: Be Direct, But Tactful

If you want something, ask for it. Most people will be more open if they understand what you want and why you want it.

Don't you just hate it when a salesperson opens a conversation by saying, "Now, I'm not here to sell you anything"? You know salespeople don't ply their trade for their health. You suspect that you will be asked for money before the person leaves, and so you resist everything that is said. At least, I do.

You can be both tactful and direct at the same time. For example, when you write a letter requesting a job interview, make your purpose your opening statement. "Dear Mr. or Ms. ————. Your friend John Smith suggested I write and ask you to grant me an interview to explain why I'm the best person available to fill your vacant position of ————. Next Friday at 2:00 P.M. would be a good time for me, but I shall be happy to come at another time if that is not convenient for you." The principle applies to every form of communication.

Tip 6: Keep the Attention of Your Audience

Assume the burden for keeping the attention of your audience. You can fix the blame on an inattentive audience, but it is always more productive to fix the problem. I like to think of the attention as if it were a telephone connection. It's foolish to keep talking once you've been disconnected.

If I've initiated a call that gets disconnected, I'll call back and wait until the person is back on the line before I begin talking again.

Unless your audience is connected to you, your messages will not get through.

Step 2: Convey Your Message
Accurately and Adequately

Since your primary goal as a responsive communicator is to obtain a desired response, let's focus our attention on how to convey messages to get results.

Again, let's turn to the pros to see how they do it. The following guidelines and pointers were collected from some of America's most successful professional speakers.

Guideline 1: Involve Your Audience

Communicating is a process, a shared experience, not simply an event. It is not enough to assume the responsibility for sending messages; you must assist your audience in receiving messages.

Remember, you want your audience to receive your message, understand it, and respond positively to it. The communication cycle is completed only when that has been accomplished.

Here are some pointers to help you involve your audience in the process from beginning to end.

Pointer 1: Listen and observe your audience constantly. Watch their expressions, their body language, and their movements. Listen to everything they say—especially their responses to what you have said.

Pointer 2: Try to build a strong trust bond. Never settle for an adversary relationship, or a we/they feeling for or from your audience. Get as close to them physically as you can, talk intimately, and use expressions such as, "You and I both know . . ." or "Together, we can . . ."

Pointer 3: Deal immediately with distractions and disturbances. Shoot for getting the most distraction-free setting possible. When people are distracted by noise or an intruder, don't just assume they'll catch up with you. Go back and pick them up, then proceed.

Pointer 4: Give them something interesting to do. A passive audience is an unreceptive audience. There's great wisdom in the following saying:

> What I hear, I forget,
> What I see, I remember,
> But what I do, I become.

Pointer 5: Value their time. Effective communicators know precisely what response they want, and they follow a carefully planned route to get it. Once they have gotten it (or it becomes clear they won't), they quit.

> If you can't prove it, don't say it.
> If you can't deliver it, don't promise it.
> If you don't agree, admit it.

Guideline 2: Say What You Mean

The pros suggest: Say what you mean, say precisely what you mean, say only what you mean. Most of us would like to do that all the time, yet we're not sure how. Their answer? Practice, practice, practice! Keep working at each of the following for as long as you want to continue improving your communication:

Pointer 1: Keep your facts straight and your opinions honest. Nothing can make people question your motives, promises, or ideas more severely than your not knowing or not telling the truth. If you can't prove it, don't say it. If you can't deliver it, don't promise it. If you don't agree, admit it. Even if people disagree strongly with you, they will respect your thoroughness and candor.

Pointer 2: Learn how to be concise. Practice constantly at cutting the fat out of your communication. As the pace of life continues to quicken, all of us will have to know how to take full advantage of the time we are allotted by our audiences.

Pointer 3: Master the fine art of plain talk. Try to use simple words, strong words, familiar words, active words. Most of all, use only words your audience will understand. That means you should avoid jargon unless you are certain your audience will understand what you mean by the terms. For example, a marine biologist talking to colleagues might say, "All the biota exhibited a mortality response." But if she were talking to a lay audience, it would be clearer for her to say, "All the fish died."

Pointer 4: Clarify misconceptions as they arise. If you finish your whole spiel, then ask if there are any questions, you may discover that your audience didn't understand anything you said because they misunderstood your opening sentence. If your audience exhibits confusion, find out what they're confused about, clear it up, then proceed.

Pointer 5: Make sure your meaning is understood, not just your words. People often hear us say what they want us to say, or what they expect us to say. For example, if I say, "I'll back you," does that mean I'll put up the money, or I'll give my moral support, or I'll defend your position, or merely that I think it's a great idea?

Guideline 3: Make It Interesting

Professional speakers think of themselves first as entertainers, then as informers or educators. That's a pretty good position for us to take in even our most routine communication attempts. Here's how they do it:

Pointer 1: Keep it lively. When you talk, be animated—move around, use gestures and facial expressions, and keep the conversation moving. Throw in a little humor, toss in some emotion, and act like it matters to you.

Pointer 2: Speak in vivid images. Many people think in images, so mental pictures can help make your messages come alive in the minds of your audience. For example, everybody knows that the wall that divides East and West Berlin is made of concrete. Yet Winston Churchill called it "the iron curtain." People all over the world have since called it that, because the words evoke a strong image that conveys a deep meaning. People love images and symbols.

Pointer 3: Use stories and illustrations. Ideas tend to be abstract, and information can be boring. Stories and illustrations are like windows; they let in light on the subject.

Pointer 4: Look for ways to connect with experiences your audience has had recently. Rodney Dangerfield has made a fortune saying, "I don't get no respect!" Why? Probably because most of us feel we don't get enough respect. Let your audience know you feel what they feel, want what they want, and fear what they fear. They'll listen a lot more closely to what you say.

Pointer 5: Make it easy to follow. Most pros suggest you use an outline of your main points so your ideas will fit together smoothly and logically. This will help your audience wade through even the most complex information. Another suggestion is to use action notes (an outline with key words left blank) and visuals to help them readily grasp difficult ideas.

Step 3: Gain the Desired Response

Responsive communicators want people to understand and agree with them, but they want more than just an empathetic hearing.

Here are some pointers from the pros on how you can more effectively stimulate people to do things.

Pointer 1: Get personal. The biggest question in the minds of most people is, "What's in it for me?" You can talk about great ideas, product features, and high-minded principles all day with little response, but you will notice your audience perk up instantly when you begin talking about how these ideas, features, and principles will benefit them. Desire is the greatest stimulus to action, and the best way to create it is to get personal about what the person stands to gain from the action you suggest.

Pointer 2: Say it with power. If you're sincere, excited, or concerned, make your audience believe you. Use strong words and say them with expression. The best way to generate enthusiasm in others is to be enthusiastic yourself.

Pointer 3: Ask confidently for the response you want. If you want people to buy, ask them to buy; if you want people to act, ask them to act. Be specific and make it clear what you want them to do. When you ask people in a vague way, to do something general, whenever they get around to it, that's the kind of response you'll get.

When you ask people in a vague way,
to do something general,
whenever they get around to it,
that's the kind of response you'll get.

Step 4: Monitor Your Results

Effective communicators never assume they have gotten the desired response—they test to make sure. Here are some ways you can do that:

Pointer 1: Plan your feedback before you communicate. It is most helpful to ask yourself not only what you want people to do, but also how you will know when they have done it. If buying means they sign an order blank, how will you get them to sign it? If you want a discordant group to come together, how will you know when they come together? It always helps to know in advance specifically how you will know you've achieved your desired response.

Pointer 2: Test understandings and intentions by asking specific questions. To simply close a meeting with the statement, "Okay, you all know what you have to do!" is to invite failure. It's much more productive to ask, "Okay, Charlie, what are you going to do?" One way to do this routinely is to briefly summarize your understandings and ask for agreement on each. An even better way is to ask members of your audience to summarize them for you.

Pointer 3: Follow up your responses. People may intend to send you a check, or do a task, or correct a mistake, but they may never get around to it. The responsive communicator looks beyond consent to completion. It's a part of keeping at it until you've accomplished your goals.

TYING IT ALL TOGETHER

Communication involves more than words; it involves exchanging meanings, values, ideas, information, and desires. You cannot communicate with a computer because it simply lacks the power to understand, to care, and to respond. Thus, communicating with other humans will always be a human task, whether you are making a date, planning a family outing, or implementing a new business strategy.

All effective communication is responsive communication—it is dialogue. The more responsive to others you are in your communication attempts, and the more you seek to obtain the response you desire from them, the better you will be able to relate to and work with people.

EIGHT

How to Set Goals for High Achievement

Our gigantic leap from the industrial society into the information age was made possible by a tiny device called a silicon chip. Futurists put it into a class with the cotton gin, the electric generator, and the light bulb.

Yet in 1961, the little chip, which had been around for several years, had a doubtful future. Most computer experts called it a "great idea, but not very practical." Although the chips had great capabilities for solving some of the biggest problems computer manufacturers had, their manufacturing cost was prohibitive—hundreds of thousands of dollars each.

But something was to happen that year that would rescue the tiny chip from oblivion and launch a process that would reshape our way of doing business, communicating with each other, and even living our daily lives. That was the year President John F. Kennedy announced that the United States would land a man on the moon before the decade was out.

Cries went up from all over the country against laying the worldwide prestige of a proud nation on the line for a clearly impossible dream. Everybody who knew anything about space technology knew that a computer capable of providing the intricate guidance system absolutely crucial to land a man on the moon would have to be as big as the

Empire State Building. There'd be no way to ever get it off the ground.

Then somebody remembered the tiny silicon chip. It had the capacity of a large computer system, and if the cost barrier could be removed, it would be more than practical. It became the only available solution.

I'm sure you know the rest of the story. In 1969, Commander Neil Armstrong took that "giant leap for mankind" on the moon's surface. The technology that made it all possible spawned an industry that now cranks out computer chips thousands of times more powerful, almost as rapidly and as cheaply as Hershey's cranks out milk chocolate Kisses. As a result, we have personal computers we can hold in our hands, robots that can perform phenomenal feats, and communications systems beyond our wildest imaginations.

Certainly, technology can be credited with giving us the tools to achieve a lunar landing, but the motivation, direction, and energy came from humans who had been challenged by a high goal. In this chapter, we will discuss (1) working together to reach high goals; (2) the benefits of setting goals; and (3) the principles of setting goals.

WORKING TOGETHER TO REACH HIGH GOALS

Nothing pulls people together for high achievement like a shared commitment to goals they feel are worthwhile, achievable, and exciting. This great nation and all its greatest institutions were built through shared commitments. Great leaders set high goals, and ordinary people have responded by working together for extraordinary achievements.

Setting goals is the way we choose how we will work with other people. It's the starting point for choosing how we will utilize all the human resources available to us, in the limited time we have.

Goal setting can be as simple as choosing to arise at a certain time each morning, or as complex as sending a man to the moon. But there are many factors that determine which goals are appropriate for us and for the people we work with.

BENEFITS OF SETTING GOALS

Responsive people have a way of getting their lives sorted out, deciding what really matters, and directing all their creative energies toward the goals they set for themselves and for the people they work with. It's a tested and proven method for high achievement, and it produces some definite benefits.

> Nothing pulls people together for high achievement like a shared commitment to goals they feel are worthwhile, achievable, and exciting.

Benefit 1: You Concentrate Your Efforts

Goals enable you to concentrate all your efforts and energies in a specific direction. Setting goals enables you to focus all the power available to you into a single focal point. It's like what happens when you hold a magnifying glass between a combustible object and the sun. That glass concentrates all the sun's rays that pass through it into a tiny spot for maximum power. If you hold it there long enough, the object will burst into flame. Concentrated power can enable you to do much more with what you have than if you simply let it wander where it will.

Benefit 2: You Make the Most of Your Time

Setting goals enables you to make the most of the time available. Each of us has only 1,440 minutes each day. You can waste them, spend them, or invest them. Whatever you put your time into each day had better be worth giving your life for, because that's exactly what you do—you trade a day of your life for it. Goals enable you to invest your life in those things that really matter to you.

Benefit 3: You Let Other People Know How to Help

Setting goals helps other people know how to help you. High achievers soon learn that they can reach their full potential only with the help of a lot of people. Many people would like to help you, but they don't know how. When you set and make known your goals, it's like giving other people handles by which they can help you carry your load.

Benefit 4: You Monitor Your Progress

Goals enable you to monitor your progress. If you don't know where you're going, how will you know when you get there? When you shoot at a target and miss it, you can determine what adjustments you need to make before the next shot. If you hit the bull's eye, you can zero in on a more challenging target.

Benefit 5: You Keep Your Enthusiasm

Goals can keep your enthusiasm, and the enthusiasm of others, at peak levels. Desire is the key to all motivation for high achievement, and nothing generates desire like an exciting goal and a strong hope of reaching it.

I like to take setting goals one step further than most people. God has shown me how to set God-sized goals, goals so high they can't be reached without His direct intervention and help. To me, that's the ultimate benefit—tapping into the full resources of the Sovereign of the universe.

PRINCIPLES FOR SETTING GOALS

Goal setting is a very crucial task when you

- Value people (including yourself) above everything but God.
- Give to people what you want to get from people.
- Make cooperation a way of life.
- Keep doing it!

Goal setting is too important a task to leave to chance. Here are some tested and proven principles to help you set goals for yourself and for the people you relate to and work with.

Principle 1: Anchor Goals in a Purpose

Peter Drucker, one of America's leading authorities on managing people, says that the most important question any organization can ask is, "What is our business?" Goals can be lofty, ideas can be great, and energy can be abundant, but if they are not anchored in a higher purpose, they will not lead us to our highest potential.

What's your purpose in life? Have you ever really sat down and taken the time to state your purpose for living, in a concise sentence? What do you believe in strongly enough to die for? What keeps you going when everything in your life flies apart? What would you like most to accomplish with your life? As you ponder these questions, your purpose will begin to emerge. Let me urge you to stay with this self-examination until you can clearly and concisely state the underlying purpose for your life—the one thing that enables you to put a foundation under all the castles you build in the air.

Once you have a clear handle on your own purpose, use the same types of questions to zero in on the purposes of the people you relate to and work with. What is the most worthwhile bond that holds you together? What will your family, friends, and coworkers give their best efforts for? What's the one thing they want most out of the relationship? It might even be helpful to ask them to help you develop a group purpose you can all support wholeheartedly.

We developed a purpose statement for our company incorporating our ideals of spirit, system, and service, and the masthead of our company's newsletter, *The Performer,* proclaims its purpose: "Dedicated to helping America's companies achieve peak performance in industrial housekeeping."

Shortly after becoming Christians several years ago, our family placed our purpose statement on a plaque and put it on our front door: "As for me and my house, we will serve the LORD" (Joshua 24:15).

In business and in the home, our decisions, actions, and investments can be fully productive only when we know where we're going. If we don't, we may be like the title character of *Alice's Adventures in Wonderland*.

"Would you tell me, please, which way I ought to go from here?" asked Alice as she stood by the side of the road.

"That depends a good deal on where you want to get to," said the Cheshire-Cat, grinning at her.

"I don't much care where —" said Alice.

"Then it doesn't matter which way you go," said the Cat.

Remember: No goal will ever rise above the purpose that gives it meaning and direction.

No goal will ever rise above
the purpose which gives it
meaning and direction.

Principle 2: Choose Goals That Are People-Oriented

All too often, people fail to reach goals because those goals are centered on sales, profits, programs, or buildings. Goals are most effective when they are centered on the needs, desires, and interests of the people who must carry them out.

During the last few decades, many leaders fell for the myth of self-motivation and the idea that you could set any goal you chose, bring in a high-powered motivational speaker to pump people up, and sit back and watch the success roll in. Recently, leaders all over the country have awakened to the fact that such tactics, at best, produce only temporary results. At worst, they make it harder and harder to get people to do anything.

A far better approach is to find out what people want and set goals that will enable them to achieve it. When people are convinced that the goals you have set will lead them to where they want to go, they will move heaven and earth to reach those goals.

Not long ago, during an interview, I was asked to name my biggest disappointment of the eleven years I've had my own business. "Without a doubt," I replied, "it's the people who have let me down." However, in all candor, I have to admit that my goals have not always been consistently people-oriented.

Remember: If you want to reach your goals, you must reach people.

People support
what they help
create.

Principle 3: Involve People in Setting Goals

People support what they help create.

"It's the computer that sets our goals. It tells us how much we must sell, for how much, and how many we must produce at what cost. From there, it's easy to know what we have to do," a modern manager may say. But don't be surprised if that same manager complains, "You just can't get an honest day's work for a good day's pay anymore."

Goals enforced from the top down usually are not met. They almost certainly won't create a climate in which people will give their best and most creative efforts.

Allowing people to participate will have a much more positive effect. Family council meetings permit everyone to contribute ideas and opinions. Sitting in on brainstorming sessions, forming task forces, filling out written surveys, and simply responding to questions verbally are some ways people can become active in the goal-setting process.

Remember: The more involved people are in setting goals, the more naturally excited they will become about reaching them.

Principle 4: Choose Appropriate Goals

As mentioned earlier, goals can be as simple as getting out of bed or as complex as putting a man on the moon. An accident victim struggling to overcome paralysis might think getting out of bed is a worthy goal, while a vigorous and resourceful nation might think putting a man on the moon is a reachable goal.

Responsive people visualize goals that stretch their resources, but not to the breaking point. Here are some of the guidelines they use:

1. Choose goals that can be reached only if people give them their best shot.
2. Choose goals that will capture the enthusiasm of the people who must fulfill them.
3. Choose relatively higher intermediate goals that will lead to your long-range goals and are within the bounds of your purpose.

Remember: If you set your goals too high, people will become easily discouraged; if you set them too low, they will not be inspired to give them their best shot.

Timetables put teeth
into your goals.

Principle 5: Choose Specific Goals

It's okay to say, "I want everybody to do his or her very best," but it is much more productive to add, "which is —-." Part of inspiring people to do their best is holding up a mirror to show them specifically what their best is.

An important part of setting goals is setting deadlines for reaching them. Timetables put teeth into your goals. For example, putting a man on the moon had been a general goal for this nation for many years, but when the president said by the end of this decade, it suddenly became a specific goal. The instruction ASAP (as soon as possible) attached to a job assignment is too open-ended because some people interpret it to mean *rush* while others interpret it to mean *when you get around to it*. As a result, there is no way for you to know when the work will be done and no way for the person receiving the message to know when you expect it. Specifying a date or a time will avoid this problem.

Remember: When you ask people to do things in a general way, when they get around to them, most people will work at them halfheartedly. But if you state specific goals, with definite deadlines, you'll be amazed at how often they are met.

Principle 6: Write Your Goals Down and Review Them Often

Writing helps to clarify a goal in your own mind and in the minds of others. Writing reinforces commitment, enables you to communicate more effectively with others, and gives you a concrete basis for monitoring. An old oriental proverb says, "The palest ink is more enduring than the strongest memory."

Also, it's a good idea to have your goals attractively displayed where everyone can see them, and to set in advance the specific times you will review them together. One year before I was to climb the Matterhorn, I hung a picture of the mountain in my office. Because I saw it there each day, and because I told many visitors to my office of my plans for the climb, my commitment to my goal deepened. Before we go on a family vacation, we find pictures of the sights we plan to see and put them on the refrigerator as constant reminders of our commitment to see them in person.

Remember: The goals you see are the goals you achieve.

Principle 7: Break Big Goals Down into Intermediate Goals

Having big, long-range goals is important, but it is hard to identify with a goal that won't come due for five years or so. All long-range goals should be broken down into manageable intermediate goals. It is even better if you can specify goals (which lead toward the long-range goal) for every day and hour. That way it is easier to relate activities to the end result.

Remember: Most people tend to procrastinate—strong intermediate goals enable you to chip away until you reach the bigger goal.

Principle 8: Take Advantage of Climbing Momentum

When you accomplish an intermediate goal on schedule, or even early, take advantage of the enthusiasm you've gen-

erated and embark immediately on the next higher intermediate goal. Because the law of inertia also affects human
beings, resting too long between reaching an intermediate
goal and climbing toward another one can cause enthusiasm to sag and actually make people feel less like climbing.

Remember: Take advantage of the momentum you have
going, and keep on climbing—even if you're way ahead of
schedule. You might even climb higher than you've dared
to dream you could.

TYING IT ALL TOGETHER

Setting goals is the way we choose how we will work
together. It's the most effective way to become a high
achiever and to lead others to high achievement.

Whether you want a new car, a stronger marriage, a re-
laxing vacation, or a more productive sales record, the same
principles and benefits apply.

As you study the principles, take a good long look at how
well your goals fit into them. You might discover some
ways to reach out for even greater achievement.

NINE

How to Plan for Responsive Action

One of the most exciting action plans I've ever been involved with came early in my business career when I was called upon to direct a major project for my local chapter of the Jaycees after I had been transferred to Mason City, Iowa. The project was called The Frite Factory, a first in Iowa, but it turned out to be more sharing than scaring.

Our stated purpose was threefold:

1. To generate enough funds to clothe needy children.
2. To reduce Halloween vandalism in our community by showing kids that somebody cared and by providing a creative form of entertainment
3. To bring chapter members and their wives together and give us an opportunity to work with one another for our community.

This purpose was rooted in our organization's underlying purpose of enabling young adults to learn how to work together to serve the community.

One of the greatest benefits I received was learning how to plan to get people to work together, to accomplish a major task, and to enjoy every minute of it. Since what I learned from The Frite Factory has been so valuable in all my workings with people, I'll use it to illustrate how planning can set the stage for action.

IT'S AMAZING WHAT YOU CAN GET DONE

Our idea was to set up and operate a haunted-house project to provide a structured activity for kids who'd otherwise be out vandalizing and to raise funds by charging admission. Did it work? Our Frite Factory project was so successful it won national recognition from the U.S. Jaycee organization.

We netted more money than expected, involved many more people than we'd dared hope for, and were received much more warmly by the entire community than we had dreamed possible. It is no exaggeration to say that The Frite Factory changed the way that community celebrated Halloween for years to come, and it influenced several other communities to turn scaring into sharing to help underprivileged children.

But how did we do it? How could a group of relatively inexperienced young men, with such limited (we thought) resources, create so much excitement in so short a time span?

Of course, a lot of credit goes to many people for major contributions, but none of that would have been possible had we not planned responsively. Let's take a closer look at how we did it, and how you can use responsive planning to get people to work together to achieve high goals.

Step 1: Break Down Purpose into
Manageable Goals

Lee Iacocca has often been quoted as saying that the key to tackling an overwhelming task is "to chip away at it."

The famous board chairman of the Chrysler Corporation has become a legend by following his own advice to salvage a major American institution from bankruptcy. His basic idea has been proven effective in some of the largest undertakings of history, yet it is simple enough to apply even to the smallest personal goals.

The first step in tackling a purpose is always to break it down into manageable goals—bite-sized chunks people can see themselves accomplishing.

It's as simple as asking and answering, "What do I have to do to make my dream come true?" It's a matter of listing what actions you need to take and what roadblocks stand in your way.

Since our Frite Factory purpose was to mobilize as many people as we could to meet the clothing needs of many of the underprivileged youngsters in our community, we set the following goals: (1) to generate $11,500 in funds by designing a haunted-house project to provide entertainment and bring in money through admissions; (2) to involve 60 Jaycees and 30 of their wives; and (3) to clothe 150 to 200 needy youngsters.

Now, to a small chapter like ours, those goals sounded mighty big, but we were convinced we could pull them off.

Next, we turned our attention to the roadblocks we'd have to overcome to make our goals become reality:

First, we'd have to gain the full backing of our officers and directors to get them to give us the up-front time and resources we'd need to make it all happen.

Second, we'd have to get the community to support the project by enlisting the aid of the city government; local businesses, schools, and organizations; and the general public.

Third, we'd have to find a suitable location—an empty building, which was structurally sound and in a good location, that could be made to look scary.

Once we had translated our purpose into manageable goals and had identified the major roadblocks, we were ready to talk about how we would make our goals happen. Had we not taken into account those roadblocks, we could have hit a snag which would have thrown the whole project off course. For example, had we not set about to gain the support of the city government, officials could have stopped the project with a zoning regulation by declaring it a "public nuisance."

Think for a moment about how you can apply this step to a project you're undertaking. How can you translate your purpose into manageable goals? What are the specific events that must take place before you can accomplish your goals? What will you have to do to get the resources you need to make it all happen? And what are the obstacles you can expect to meet along the way?

When you can satisfactorily answer those questions, you have a starting point. Goals are like handles—they give you something solid to grab hold of and work with.

Most great achievements of history were not accomplished by superhumans, they were accomplished by people who were willing to chip away at big purposes by breaking them down into goals and tasks they could do.

That brings us to the next big step in planning for responsiveness.

Step 2: Develop Strategies

A strategy is nothing more than a plan to accomplish a goal or overcome a roadblock. Unresponsive people stand around and complain, "People just don't understand the need for what I'm proposing to do." But responsive people ask, "How can I make people see the value in it?"

One of the most valuable lessons I ever learned about working with people is that they seldom do things for my reasons; they have their own reasons. Therefore, whether I want to launch a civic project, sell someone a product or service, build a corporation, have my kids take piano lessons, talk my wife into another mountain climb, or raise money to build a hospital, my challenge is always to show others how my proposal will meet their needs, desires, and interests. Once I've shown them how to get what they want, they almost run over me to get it.

That principle is the key to responsive planning and developing strategies for acting together.

The K.I.S.M.I.F. Principle

You'll constantly be amazed at how much you can get people to do when you learn how to create a desire in them to do it.

Stanley Bond retired many years ago from an executive position with Firestone Tire and Rubber Company in Akron, Ohio, but he was a long way from being finished in making his contributions. He continued to work as the volunteer superintendent of Akron Baptist Temple until it could boast of having the largest Sunday school in America—with an average attendance of more than 9,500.

A reporter, noticing that most of the work was being done by volunteers, asked the aging administrator how he had been able to get so many people to do so much for no pay.

"We use the K.I.S.M.I.F. principle," he replied with a gleam in his eye.

"What in the world is that?" asked the reporter.

"It stands for *Keep It Simple, Make It Fun,*" came the reply.

The best strategies are simple. They're not the kinds of things that only a genius can do, but are the kinds of things an average person, with modest resources, can do in a relatively short time.

As project coordinator of The Frite Factory, I developed

strategies the Jaycee officers could easily do, such as giving me time in the meetings to present the project to the members, appointing people to help secure a location, going with our committee to talk to city officials, and helping us negotiate with business and civic leaders. Once the Jaycee officers understood what was expected of them, and that it was easily within their grasp, they were enthusiastic about helping.

There's not space here to talk about all the strategies we developed to make the project click, but I hope you get the idea. The whole project was put together by developing strategies to fulfill every goal and to overcome every obstacle.

Step 3: Set Priorities

One reason many of us find it so hard to get things done, and always feel like we're being run to death, is that we have not learned to distinguish what is urgent from what is important.

Urgencies scream for our attention, they keep us running around in circles, and they sap our most creative energies. Yet they seldom seem as crucial in the long run as they seem at the moment.

If you're caught up in responding to the urgent in your life, one of the best ways to overcome it is to try to remember what it was that made you run like crazy one year ago today. What was the long-term impact of a machine that didn't run right, or a person who didn't show up for work, or a problem that seemed to overwhelm you? Chances are pretty good you can't even remember what it was that drove you up a wall just one year ago today.

The tragedy of it all is that the urgencies often keep us from doing what's important. Responsive leaders learn how to separate the urgent from the important and to con-

> Chances are pretty good you can't even remember
> what it was that drove you up a wall
> just one year ago today.

centrate their energies on what really matters. They learn to identify priorities and take care of them first.

Interestingly, when you learn to concentrate your greatest resources on priorities, urgencies seem to have a way of getting handled—or maybe they just don't come up as often.

Here are some questions you can use to help you sort through tasks to separate out the priorities:

1. What are the most essential elements to getting the job done? In other words, what are the few absolutely crucial tasks that must be done?
2. What will be the long-term effect of this task getting done or not getting done?
3. What is the relationship of this task to the other tasks you need to be working on? If this task doesn't get done, will it be as bad as if another task doesn't get done?
4. Do you have to do it right now to take care of it?
5. Is the urgency something that can be handled by someone else so you can concentrate upon something more important?

One very helpful approach to setting priorities is listing all the tasks that you (and the people you're working with) must get done and assigning a priority level to each. Priority level one would be those things that absolutely must get done. Level two would be the next level of importance, and so on in descending order.

Once you have established priorities, start with those designated level one and, once you have either done them or provided for them to be done, move on down the list.

It's a simple technique, which can take a few minutes out of every day but can save you valuable hours and even days in pulling off a big project.

Step 4: Set Timetables and Schedules

When you work with people, time is your most valuable asset. If you use your time and their time wisely, it can work for you; if you squander it, time (or the lack of it) can drive you up a wall.

The most crucial element in utilizing the time and resources you have available is to set up a timetable and schedule for everything that must happen.

Our first priority in getting The Frite Factory off the ground was selling our officers and directors on the idea. So the project committee set up a definite time when we would meet with them, and we planned how we would accomplish that goal in the time we had available.

But we didn't wait until we had done that to set up our next deadline. We set up a schedule for contacting every resource we would need, and we determined deadlines for having the facility secured, all our committees in place, and the construction of the scary scenes completed. We planned in advance when and how we would evaluate what we had done and how we would follow up the project.

Our schedule became a map that enabled us to know exactly when each person needed to be doing what. Instead of restricting us (as some feared it would), our schedule gave us freedom to have fun along the way. By knowing that all the work would get done, we enjoyed the journey.

Step 5: Plan Your Evaluation

Planning your project evaluation enables you to get feedback as you go along. Periodic evaluations along the way enable you to make adjustments, and they give you and the other people involved an immediate look at and a long-term projection of how everything is working out.

One of the most valuable questions you can ask at the beginning of a project is, "What will success look like?" The answer to that question leads to other valuable questions: Who's going to be responsible for what? And how will I know it's done? How can we tell what adjustments need to be made to make up for lost time? What worked and didn't work? How could we have avoided problems we encountered?

> One of the basic human emotional needs
> is for recognition and reward.

This question-and-answer procedure is a little like an airline pilot planning where he or she will land before taking off. Planning will tell how much fuel will be needed, how long the trip will take, and what other vital information will be required to assure a successful flight.

Step 6: Plan for Celebration

The responsive leader never relies on the old adage about virtue being its own reward. Those who are really successful at getting others to do things know that one of the basic human emotional needs is for recognition and reward. They know that people need the camaraderie of celebrating their achievements together.

Thus, responsive leaders always plan in advance how they will enable the group to celebrate its victories and how individuals will be rewarded for the specific contributions they have made.

For example, we knew that people would naturally feel some sense of reward at knowing they had helped to provide clothing for needy children. So we wanted to make sure that everyone who participated in The Frite Factory was involved in the distributing of the coats, hats, shoes, and other items purchased with the proceeds from our collective efforts. At the same time, we wanted to protect the feelings of the children and their parents. We planned very carefully how the clothing would be distributed, how our members would be made to feel a part of it, and how we finally would celebrate with the Appreciation Night Banquet.

WHEN SCARING TURNED TO SHARING

Planning and running The Frite Factory was my first big taste of the exciting challenge of leading a large group of people to high achievement. Not only did we meet our goals, we surpassed them.

1. We were able to get everybody in our chapter actively involved, and we obtained many more volunteer hours than we'd hoped for.

2. Instead of the 30 wives we wanted to involve, we were able to involve 57 wives, and other people as well.

3. Our goal was to raise $11,500, and we raised a total of $10,740. Since our expenses were lower than we had ex-

pected, however, our net was actually better than we'd projected.

4. We mobilized 183 high school and college young people to help us, and we introduced our organization to many potential members.

5. Some 24 local merchants donated more than $1500 worth of goods and services. A local radio station agreed to be a joint sponsor with us and gave us untold publicity.

6. Perhaps most important, we were able to provide a heavy winter coat, a shirt, a pair of jeans, a pair of shoes, and a hat for each of 190 needy youngsters just before Christmas.

In all, the project was so successful that the chapter decided to adopt The Frite Factory as an annual event.

On a personal level, The Frite Factory taught me that you can get a lot more commitment, creative energy, and cooperation out of people by giving them an opportunity to *share* themselves with each other—and with others—than by trying to *scare* them into doing what you expect them to do. This experience has shaped my whole outlook on working with people in our company, with our clients, and even with audiences in the seminars and speeches I give.

TYING IT ALL TOGETHER

If you want to be a responsive leader of people, let me urge you to learn how to plan responsively and to learn how to give people a framework from which they can work together to achieve goals that are important to them.

Plan one step at a time, and you'll fulfill your purpose: *goals* (what do you want?); *strategies* (how do you get there?); *priorities* (what is most important?); *timetables* (when does what need to get done?); *evaluation* (how will

---

You can get a lot more commitment, creative energy,
and cooperation out of people by giving them
an opportunity to *share* themselves with each other
—and with others—than by trying to *scare* them into
doing what you expect them to do.

---

you know when you've achieved your goals?); and *celebration* (how will you reward yourself and the other people involved?).

TEN

How to Choose and Channel People for High Achievement

Every coach in the National Football League knows that chances are pretty good he'll have to climb over the Miami Dolphins on the road to winning the Super Bowl, and that's no easy task. Don Schula, the Dolphins' head coach, has a reputation for putting together a perennial powerhouse of a team.

Players, colleagues, and sports journalists agree that what makes Coach Shula so effective is that he is a master at choosing and channeling people to build a winning team. He has cultivated the ability to pick players to fit the skills of his other players, to know where each player can do his best, and then to motivate each person to do his best.

PRINCIPLES THAT GUIDE RESPONSIVE LEADERS

In this chapter, let's look at some of the underlying principles that guide the legendary coach and many other responsive leaders who have learned how to work with people for high achievement.

Principle 1: Choose People Whose Goals Are Compatible with Yours

A coach cannot build a winning team with a bunch of players whose only goal is to make it into the professional leagues. This truth extends to every area of working with people. You can reach your personal goals only when you systematically surround yourself with people whose goals are compatible with yours.

You may have noticed that I used the term *compatible with*, as opposed to saying *the same as* yours. It is quite possible that people with different, but compatible, goals can work together successfully. Their differences may even complement each other.

For example, a doctor's primary goal might involve providing the best medical care available for a community, but he or she might lack the resources to do it. A hospital administrator's primary goal might involve building and running a top-notch facility. By working together, they can mesh their goals to provide good medical care, at reasonable prices, and with a solid financial base.

When you are selecting a team, or members for an existing team, it is always a good idea to start with people who are motivated to work toward compatible goals.

Principle 2: Choose People Who Fit Your Team

Each new person you bring into a team changes the mix and changes the way the whole team functions. Whether this works for you or against you depends on your selection process.

Hiring a person on raw talent alone may destroy the mix you're trying to build. The most important question is always, "How well can this person work with the rest of the team?"

Interestingly, more and more major corporations are beginning to list a demonstrated ability to work effectively with people as the first qualification for a new chief executive officer.

Now, this does not suggest that you hire only those people who are friendly and outgoing. It is not enough that a person be able to get along well with others—that person must be able to get others to do things.

Ideally, each new person should give the team a new dimension of capability.

It is not enough that a person be able
to get along well with others
—that person must be able to get others
to do things.

Principle 3: Look for Skills and Strengths You Need

Conflicts can be avoided, morale boosted, and overall effectiveness increased by choosing people who can fill voids.

The old adage that a good manager can manage anything, or that a good salesperson can sell anything, is being challenged by an increasing number of administrators. The question always revolves around whether or not a person has the skills and strengths to do the specific task you need done.

Responsive leaders always ask the question, "What sort of person do we need to do this task?" The best way to answer that question is to do a thorough analysis of the task to be done and to try to visualize a person actually doing it.

A key criterion for fitting a person to a task is finding out if the person enjoys doing the kinds of things that will be expected. If the task is enjoyable, the performance is likely to be good.

One tool used effectively by many leaders is a needs priority listing. They'll draw up a list of skills and strengths the person "must have." Then they'll list skills and strengths it would be "nice to have." Finally, they'll list skills and strengths that are "not assets" for a specific position. As a result, they can be more objective in their final selection process. The candidates who have the most of the "must haves" and the "nice to haves" get first consideration.

During the early years of being in the employment market to fill positions in our firm, we based our decisions primarily on a resume, employment application, interview, and the firmness of the handshake. After disappointing turnover of personnel and things just not working out sometimes, we decided to work smarter in our employee selection process. The first step was to analyze every position in terms of the strengths needed and arrive at a profile of the person who would be successful in the position. Then, we began to systematically evaluate each applicant through the use of resume, employment application, personality assessment tools, interviews with questions targeted at the applicant's weaknesses, and references, and to determine how the individual would complement those who were already employees or who would be members of the newly formed team. We selected our management employees based on the known high probability that they would succeed.

The results have been very gratifying not only for the corporation but also for the people we employ. There are few things more enjoyable for an employee than to be in a position of being able to offer what the job requires. What a launching pad from which to grow and develop personally! And what harvestable fields it provides from which a corporation can feed its expansion!

Principle 4: Base Promotions on Ability

Many excellent workers have been destroyed by being promoted to a position of authority simply because they have done a good job. A skilled worker not only may be a lousy supervisor but also may hate the job.

Responsive leaders look for other ways to reward those who do a good job at one level. It may be flattering to an employee to be promoted to supervisor, but the end result may not be seen as a reward at all.

Admittedly, this can be an explosive principle—especially when unions are involved—but the responsive leader constantly searches for ways of dealing with it.

One effective technique is to involve as many people as possible in making the decision about who will fill a newly vacated or created position. Another valuable aid is to anticipate upcoming promotions and seek to prepare people for jobs they will be called upon to do at some future time. Still another aid is to sell constantly the team-approach idea and to cultivate team players.

Most leaders in the human resources field agree that this principle will become increasingly important the further we move toward a high-tech environment.

Principle 5: Channel People by Their Strengths

Some of the most capable people in industry and commerce never utilize their greatest strengths. They may be locked into what management considers an important job, and they may do it well. But they may never get an opportunity to do what they can do best.

When this happens, everybody loses. The person loses because of lack of opportunity and lack of job satisfaction; the organization loses because it wastes some of its most valuable assets; and the whole venture operates at less than capacity.

One way to avoid this loss is to ask probing questions: "What can this person do best?" "Are we utilizing this person's greatest strengths?" and "How can we better take advantage of the talents this person can bring to us?" In our corporation we seek the answers to all these questions through the continued use of the information we get in our employee selection process. We counsel with our employees and talk specifically about their strengths and weaknesses. If they are channeled into new areas, they have the advantage of knowing why. And, similarly, they know why they may not be channeled into certain areas.

Principle 6: Monitor Effectiveness— Not Just Action

Responsive leaders realize that motion is not always progress, and that action is not always effectiveness. The big question is not, "How hard does this person work?" but, "How much does this person get done?"

An old school of thought said that a person who was not getting the job done was just goofing off. More and more smart leaders are taking the view that any person who is not getting the job done is basically a management problem—he or she is not being managed properly.

Another tenet of the old school was that the best way to manage people was to set standards for each job classification, then monitor each worker in relation to those standards. But many leaders are awakening to the fact that operating on that theory drives some people up the walls and allows others to coast along. Today's alert manager

172

asks what each person is capable of doing, and strives to keep him or her functioning at an optimum level.

Principle 7: Promote Time Management at All Levels

A supervisor walks through a department and shouts, "Hurry up, every chance you get!" While he's there, you'll see a flurry of activity. But when he leaves, the pace slackens noticeably.

Good time management is much more than simply working faster—it's working smarter. A person might be quite busy most of the time doing things that aren't really all that important. Even the trusted "to-do" list can create a trap of busywork if it is used to keep yourself or others doing insignificant chores. Some people get such an emotional lift out of crossing off tasks from their lists that they pad those lists with "trivial pursuits." At the end of the day, they look at their lists and see all the things that are checked off and say they've had a productive day.

> Good time management is much more
> than simply working faster
> —it's working smarter.

To-do lists and work-flow schedules are excellent time-management tools, but only if they are built around your goals and objectives. It is a good idea to close each day with a recap of your list to see how many of your priorities for that day were accomplished. Then it's helpful to make your list for the next day on the basis of your highest priorities.

Some leaders prioritize their to-do lists and encourage everyone they work with to do the same. They select the two, three, or four things they consider most important for them to get done the next day. Then they assign the most important task a number one priority and rate the remaining tasks in descending order. As much as possible, they start with their highest priority first thing in the morning and work down the list in descending order.

Promoting good time management is a constant process, and strategies include:

1. Keep a work diary to see what kinds of activities eat up your time, and encourage others to do the same.
2. Seek to discover what times of the day are most productive, and schedule your highest priority tasks to be done when you are at your best.
3. Handle paperwork instead of just shuffling papers. One of the best time managers I know has a rule that he will handle each piece of paper only one time. He can't always live by that rule, but you'd be amazed at how much time he saves by disposing of each piece of paper as it comes up.
4. Organize your desk or work station. One busy executive almost passed out when a time-management consultant proved to him that he averaged spending more than two hours each day just looking for things on his desk and in his files. The catch was that the time was wasted a few minutes at a time, so the loss was not apparent. He immediately reorganized his whole office.
5. Constantly look for ways to do things more effectively. Almost everything we do can be improved upon, and the more often we do a task, the greater the necessity to find more effective ways of getting it done.
6. Constantly observe habits. Most of us tend to do the easy, quick, pleasant, and urgent things before we jump on the tough assignments with higher priorities. The

best way to break time-wasting habits is to cultivate new time-investing habits centered on your priorities.

7. Eliminate time-wasting traps. Lingering too long at the vending machines, talking with someone a few extra minutes here and there, and twiddling your thumbs while you're waiting for someone can eat up massive amounts of time—one minute at a time.

The point of this time-management principle is that a big part of channeling people is channeling them into *productive* activities. Promoting good time-management habits is one of the highest priorities of responsive leadership.

Principle 8: Become a Master at Delegating

The idea that "the only way to get something done right is to do it yourself" is a relic from the past that does little more than stroke the ego of a person who wants to feel indispensable. Oddly enough, the people who think that way often become very dispensable.

One reason so many people are reluctant to give authority to others is that they feel they are giving up something that rightfully belongs to them. When you give people the authority they need to get a job done, you're not giving up anything—you're merely sharing the responsibility with another person.

Another reason some leaders hesitate to delegate is that they are afraid others will make them look bad to their superiors. Responsive leaders realize that nothing makes them look worse than failing to lead others to high achievement.

Some definite techniques that effective delegators find useful include:

1. Give clear instructions, and make sure the person understands precisely what is expected.
2. Make clear the priority you place on the task.
3. Provide all the resources the person needs to get the job done.
4. Develop a system for delegating authority levels. The following guide can help you see how it works:

    Level 1: Study the situation and report to me; I'll make the decision.

    Level 2: Study the situation and make a recommendation to me; I'll decide what action to take.

    Level 3: Study the situation and choose a course of action; don't act until I've approved.

    Level 4: Handle the situation and advise me of what you did.

    Level 5: Handle the situation; you need not advise me of what you did.

    Of course, you will determine the levels of authority by such factors as the subordinate's experience and expertise, the complexity of the task, the time available, and the amount of responsibility you can entrust to the person. But using such a system can eliminate a lot of confusion about what's expected.
5. Make clear to all concerned what level of authority you're giving the person. One reason many people fail to follow through with an assignment is that they don't want to make others feel they're throwing their weight around.
6. Hold people accountable for their actions. Remember, when you delegate authority to act, you don't abdicate your responsibility to get the job done. If the people to whom you delegate responsibility fail, the end result is that your leadership has failed. That means you have the right and responsibility to hold people accountable.

Reporting methods can be as complex as detailed written reports and as simple as a nonverbal signal that the job is done. As a rule, the best approach is to use the simplest method you can to determine three things:

1. Is satisfactory progress being made toward fulfilling the task?
2. Are the resources adequate to finish the job on schedule?
3. Are the resources being used effectively and efficiently?

When people know what you expect and know that they will have to give an account of their actions, they tend to enjoy the trust that delegation implies. Thus, they will usually knock themselves out to get the job done for you.

Principle 9: Be Willing to Make Changes

As carefully as you may try to channel people for maximum performance, sometimes you will find you have a person in the wrong slot. People change, jobs change, and even the most astute leaders occasionally make miscalculations in determining a person's strength, expertise, and level of commitment.

The responsive leader is constantly alert to see that each person is in a position to do his or her best for the total team effort. If you discover that a person has strengths you hadn't noticed, or if you spot weaknesses that hamper a person's effectiveness, move quickly to shift the person to a new position where he or she can perform at a more efficient level.

Of course, tact is the key to all such moves. If possible, make the decision to change a person's role a compliment to their abilities. For example, if you have a salesperson who's doing poorly, you might say, "I've noticed that you are very strong on detail work, and we have an important detail-oriented job open. Would you like to make a change?"

Moving people from one slot to another can be unsettling to them and to others around them. Make sure that you study the situation carefully to ensure that the change will result in improved performance and that you adequately prepare everyone for the change.

Principle 10: Smile and Make Clear What You Expect

The combination of clear-cut expectations and a smile can work wonders in channeling people for high achievement. Alone, neither will get the job done.

> The combination of clear-cut expectations and a smile can work wonders in channeling people for high achievement.

Recent studies have shown that managers who bark out orders like drill sergeants, growl at everybody, and seem to enjoy making people look insignificant seldom get peak performance out of subordinates. Similarly, managers who simply smile and assume that people know what is wanted often get even less.

However, managers who treat subordinates with dignity and respect and who make clear what they expect tend to bring out the best in people.

A good example of this is how different managers approach salary increases. Some managers smile, commend the workers, and congratulate them on deserving more money. Other managers grumble about having to give increases, sound as if they're putting the employees on probation, and act as if they're doing them a great big favor. It doesn't cost a dime more to give a smile along with the raise, but the consequent difference in performance level can be dramatic.

TYING IT ALL TOGETHER

Responsiveness in working with people means that you select and channel people so they can give peak performances constantly. But how does that relate to the four components of the Dynamic Responsiveness System of working with people?

First, it means you value people enough to put them into only those slots where they can reach their full potential as creatures of God. Second, it means you make available to others the kinds of opportunities you'd like most to have for yourself. Third, it means you cooperate with others by channeling them into areas that match their strengths, needs, and interests. And fourth, it means you keep working at increasing each person's sense of fulfillment in doing the tasks you assign.

Leading and channeling your family and friends to high performance is no different from leading people you work with. In personal relationships, of course, you won't be so concerned with paperwork as you will be concerned with verbal communication. The important point is that expectations be clear and that ambiguity be eliminated.

That leads us to the next important skill for responsive leadership—equipping people for high achievement.

ELEVEN

How to Equip People for High Achievement

Each time I have set out to assault one of the high mountains of the world, I've been asked one question by the local climbers: "Do you want to climb fully equipped, or the hard way?" I learned very early in my mountain climbing experiences why they phrase the question that way.

Climbing *fully equipped* means you hire expert guides to lead you to the mountain peak by the best route, outfitters to provide the essential equipment you need for a good climb, and bearers to carry the provisions for you.

But climbing *the hard way* means going it alone—with no one to show you the way, with no equipment other than what you can carry on your back, and with no outside aid in times of emergency. Believe me, it is the hard way, and the most dangerous.

One of the primary tasks in working responsively with people is enabling them to climb toward high achievement fully equipped. In this chapter we want to take a look at three essentials for responsive leaders. Responsive leaders (1) give expert guidance; (2) make available adequate resources; and (3) eliminate unnecessary burdens.

GIVE EXPERT GUIDANCE

The Matterhorn is no mountain to be taken lightly. This mammoth rock towers 14,780 feet into the sky and casts an almost eerie spell over the little village of Zermatt, Switzerland, which nestles at its base. Its jagged overhang juts out into space, its icy slopes and ledges glisten mockingly in the sun, and the bone-chilling winds that whistle around it groan like air raid sirens. Everything about this giant obelisk, called the tiger of the Alps, spells DANGER.

As I stood gazing up at that formidable living rock, I knew I'd have to give it my best shot to have any hope of reaching its peak. But I also knew I couldn't do it alone. One wrong choice of route, one distracted misstep, or one slight miscalculation could easily mean the end of John Noe.

I needed an expert guide—one who'd been where I wanted to go, one who knew the best and safest routes to get there, and one who knew something about leading people. Alfons Franzen had a worldwide reputation of being just such a guide.

And when I met him, it didn't take long for me to understand why he had such a reputation. He seemed to look right through my eyes to see what I was made of. He tested me more severely than I'd ever been tested, and he sized up everything I did. Finally, he said, "Well, John, it's going to be difficult for you, but I think we can make it together."

As it turned out, he was right on both counts. We did make it all the way to the top and back down (the most dangerous part of a climb), and to call it difficult is to make a gross understatement.

But I came away from that major climb with a new appreciation for the word *guide*. I was so impressed with his expertise and leadership abilities that I decided expert guides were absolutely essential in every area of my life, including my business life.

What's more, I decided to become a guide for others in areas in which I had expertise and skills. Leading people to high achievement has been such an exciting adventure that I often wish I had started following and being a guide much earlier in my life.

Let's take a look at some of the things expert guides provide.

Provision 1: Expert Guides Give Leadership

To lead means "to go in front to show the way." If you are considered to be an expert guide, the implications are that you've been where the person you're leading wants to go, that you know the way, and that you're willing to point out the best ways to reach a cherished goal.

Leading others means that you set the pace for them to follow. You set an example for them to emulate, you urge them on when they begin to falter, and you give them hope that they can make it.

> Good leadership is not so much a matter
> of demanding performance as it is
> inspiring enthusiasm.

Leadership also means disciplining those who follow you. You warn them of pitfalls and give guidance toward safer ground, you correct them when they make mistakes, and you constantly give pointers of better ways to do things.

Good leaders always give their best and expect others to do the same. Good leadership is not so much a matter of demanding performance as it is inspiring enthusiasm.

Provision 2: Expert Guides Are Good Teachers

Expert guides understand that what they know so well, others may not know at all. They never assume that people know how to do what's expected. Rather, they test to make sure what people know.

Good leaders enable others to understand the roles they're expected to play, the functions they're expected to perform, and the goals they're expected to achieve.

Responsive leaders are always willing to take the time to give instructions and, if necessary, give them again and again until they're understood.

Provision 3: Expert Guides Are Good Trainers

Expert guides know that the best way to learn many things is to do them, so they constantly conduct on-the-job training sessions.

Good leaders also know that mastery of skills takes practice, so they give their followers opportunities to try, to fail, and to try again.

Confidence often determines effectiveness. Expert guides know this, so they work hard at building competence in others to such a level that they feel confident they can do what's expected of them.

Provision 4: Expert Guides Make Following Others a Way of Life

If you would be successful in working with other people, one of the basics you must provide is guidance, constant guidance. To do this, you must constantly seek out and follow your own expert guides who can show you better ways to lead others. That means it's a good idea to read frequently, to listen carefully, and to observe how other professionals do it.

MAKE AVAILABLE ADEQUATE RESOURCES

Each mountain has its own personality and poses its unique challenge. Mount Kilimanjaro is as different from the Matterhorn as daylight is from dark. Someone compared climbing Kilimanjaro to climbing a staircase two miles long. When you add the temperature swings of 90 degrees each day, the almost-unbreathably thin air at 19,340 feet, the slog through the scree (ankle-deep lava gravel and dust) on the mountain's peak, and the threatening winds and snows, it can quickly reduce a man in his prime to the capacity of a sickly and feeble old man.

My wife, Cindy, who accompanied me on that climb, and I knew that just getting to the top of that mountain would take all we could do. We certainly didn't need to concern ourselves with securing the equipment we would need, doing our own cooking, and taking care of our own housekeeping. We needed an outfitter who would take care of all that for us so we could concentrate on what we had come to Africa to achieve. In the five days and four nights that climb took, we learned how valuable a good outfitter can be.

Responsive leaders know how important it is to make available all the resources people need to be able to function at peak performance. They know that sending a person out to do a job without adequate resources is like sending a paperhanger out with one hand tied behind him. If he's a hero, he will get the job done regardless of the handicaps. But no matter how good he is, it will take a lot longer.

Good leaders always make available to their followers the

resources needed to get the job done as quickly and effectively as possible. Those resources include several essentials.

Resource 1: A Clearly Defined Task

We've talked about this in other settings, but it is important enough to at least mention here. Smart leaders know that one of the greatest resources for getting a job done is a clear understanding of what that job is, and how it can be done effectively.

Did you notice I used the word *effectively?* There is often a vast difference in doing things *efficiently* and doing them *effectively*. It may be efficient for a quality control inspector to simply overlook flaws in products, but it is certainly not very effective.

The good leader makes sure that people are as effective as possible by ensuring that they know not only what to do but also the most effective way to do it.

Resource 2: A Productive Environment

It is no more shortsighted to select ineffective people than it is to give effective people unproductive environments to work in.

When we talk about a work environment, the tendency is to jump to the conclusion that we're calling for soft lights, beautiful surroundings, and stereo music. That may not be a productive environment at all. The bottom line is always what kind of environment it takes to make people as effective as possible.

One of the hazards of our high-tech world is fully integrated offices and plants that are very difficult for people to work in. You can buy the latest equipment, arrange it according to the most efficient layouts, and control the temperature and humidity to perfect levels. But if the people who must work in that facility have to squint to see, sit in uncomfortable positions, or struggle to stay awake, don't be surprised if the work flow slows down and mistakes occur more often.

Good leaders know that providing adequate resources includes creating a climate in which people can work most effectively and productively.

Resource 3: The Right Equipment

Many leaders seem to pride themselves on how much they get done with very little, often outmoded, equipment. As a result, they expect the people they work with to get by with little or nothing by way of equipment. "We prefer to put our money into salaries so we can get the best people," they like to boast.

Other leaders seem to go to the other extreme. They've got to have at least one of every new gadget that comes along.

Responsive leaders fall somewhere between those two extremes. Their primary goal is to get the job done most effectively and efficiently, and they are aware that the right tools can often make the difference in an employee's effectiveness and efficiency.

The explosion in technology offers tremendous opportunities for making people more productive, and yet it poses tough questions about what equipment to buy. You buy state-of-the-art equipment this year, only to find out that next year there's a new state-of-the-art. In fact, it's not unusual for a piece of major equipment to be outmoded before it's installed.

Smart leaders know that the key question is always, "What equipment will make the person most productive, for the least investment?" They think in terms of cost-effectiveness ratios on a long-term basis.

Responsive leaders also know that the people who must operate the equipment can give the best input regarding which equipment will make them most productive. Before any decision is final, they consult with those who will run the equipment. Of course, a wide variety of factors usually precludes leaving the final decision entirely with the operators, but it is always a good idea to ask their opinions before a decision is made.

Henry Ford, the automobile pioneer, is supposed to have used a variation of this approach. It is reported that when he had a difficult or time-consuming task to be done, he'd search out the "laziest" person in his plant to do it. His theory was that the lazier a person, the quicker an easier way to do the job could be found. That may be a little extreme, but the principle is good. The people who do the job most often give valuable input.

Providing the right equipment suggests another concern—that the equipment be in proper working order. Most equipment is designed to operate at an optimum level. And if it is not kept in good working order, it will not run efficiently, nor will it make the worker productive.

Probably the most commonly overlooked concern in having the right equipment is making sure the person knows how to operate it well. I am constantly dismayed at how many production-conscious managers will spend big money buying equipment, then refuse to invest either time or money to properly train those who must operate it.

To neglect training is a little like the woodlot operator who hired the fastest woodcutter he'd ever seen. To get the full benefit of the fellow's skills, the woodlot operator replaced the ax with a chain saw. "I'll bet he can cut three cords of wood a day," the operator boasted to a colleague.

Upon returning to the lot late in the afternoon, the operator discovered that the woodcutter had cut only a single cord of wood, yet he was lying beside the pile exhausted. "What's wrong?" he asked.

"I want my ax back. That thing won't half cut!" said the woodcutter.

"Why, this chain saw is the best money can buy," he challenged. "Let's see what's wrong." He walked over, switched on the saw, and pulled the cord. The saw let out a tremendous roar.

"What's that noise?" shouted the surprised woodcutter.

The moral of the story is that if you want peak performance out of a piece of equipment, make sure the person who must operate it knows how to operate it properly.

Special note: This discussion has centered on paid workers in the business environment. But everything said here can be doubly important when working with volunteers. Unfortunately, many effective volunteers available to nonprofit organizations get discouraged and drop out because everything they're asked to do, they're asked to do without the resources to get it done right.

A great challenge faced by responsive leaders in volunteer organizations is enabling people to work fully equipped. Nothing requires greater creativity, more ingenuity, and more enduring patience than seeking out and providing proper resources. Yet nothing can produce greater effectiveness and rewards.

Whether you're working with volunteers, professionals, or hourly workers, the major concern is making sure that people have the right equipment, that the equipment works properly, and that operators know how to use it effectively and efficiently.

ELIMINATE UNNECESSARY BURDENS

When Cindy and I set out to climb Mount Kilimanjaro, our primary goal was to reach its lofty peak. We were not out to prove how self-sufficient, physically fit, or tough we

188

were. We had seen that peak which, on a clear day, is visible for more than a hundred miles. We wanted to view the world from its vantage point.

I cannot tell you how exhilarating it was to reach the top, to drink in the total silence, and to look a hundred miles in every direction over the top of Africa. It was everything we'd dreamed of, and more.

Yet both of us realized that we never could have made it if we'd had to carry all our own provisions. Reaching our goal depended upon our willingness to save our energies for our highest priority—climbing.

Excess baggage causes people to operate
far below their capabilities.

That experience taught me a lot about working responsively with people. Primarily, it taught me that I can lead people to peak performance only when I am willing to eliminate their unnecessary burdens. Excess baggage causes people to operate far below their capabilities.

Let's look at some of that excess baggage the responsive leader eliminates to lead people to peak performance.

Excess Baggage Item 1: Unnecessary Tasks

Few of us would be so foolish as to ask a brain surgeon to mop up the floor after an operation. Yet we can easily fall into traps that are just as wasteful of the skills and time of very capable people.

Unnecessary paperwork is one of the most common wasters of valuable time people have to contend with. Reports that are not needed, files that are never opened, and memos that accomplish nothing have forced us into fleeing to computers to store all that information. Now we have computer printouts nobody needs or uses, operators who spend endless hours making entries that never will be called for, and high-cost overnight letters that will sit on somebody's desk for days before being opened.

Effective leaders know that often the most important question to ask about each report, memo, or letter is, "Is it really necessary?" If the answer to that question comes up yes, the second most important question becomes, "What's the quickest, easiest, most economical, and most effective way for people to produce it, send it, and utilize it?"

Most time-management specialists agree that dealing properly with those two questions can result in a 10 to 15 percent increase in productivity for the average worker in American business.

Unnecessary meetings—and poorly conducted meetings—run a close second to paperwork in wasting valuable time of capable people.

Meetings alone waste enough time, but when you add the time spent in preparation, the time spent traveling to and from meetings, and the salaries of people in the meetings, the cost in human resources is staggering.

Eliminating unnecessary meetings and holding productive ones is so important that we will devote a whole chapter to it later. Here, let me simply say that any effort you can make at assuring that valuable people don't waste time on meetings will be energy well spent.

Busywork is another unnecessary task that holds people back from peak performance. The manager who operates on the basis that people have to be paid anyway so let's give them something to do, or that giving certain tasks to people makes them feel important, is guilty of poor planning.

Many leaders fall into that trap because they are so busy with unnecessary tasks themselves that they have no time for planning.

190

Just as in dealing with paperwork and useless meetings, eliminating busywork revolves around two questions: "Is this task necessary to accomplish our goals?" and "What's the quickest, easiest, and most effective way to get it done?"

Excess Baggage Item 2: Disturbances and Distractions

You'd probably be shocked at how much time people lose because they are interrupted unnecessarily. The worker who pops into the boss's office to ask a trivial question at an inopportune moment, the boss who drops by a work station to tell somebody something before he or she forgets, the uninvited visitor who drops by for a chat—all these and many more eat up time with a vengeance.

Without a doubt, the greatest eliminator of this excess baggage item is careful planning. A closer look at one crucial area—telephone usage—can serve to illustrate how planning can help to eliminate distractions and disturbances.

> Whether you control your telephone,
> or allow it to control you,
> depends on how much planning
> goes into the system.

Whether you control your telephone, or allow it to control you, depends on how much planning goes into your system. Here are some planning tips to help you get control of this time waster:

1. Plan to use the phone at certain times of the day, and only then. As offensive as it is to some people, most time-conscious contacts realize the necessity of bunching calls—making and returning calls in a given time frame.
2. Plan each call before you make it. Make a list of the major points you want to cover, and stick to only those.
3. Collect everything you'll need to accomplish your purpose in calling. Pen, paper, documents, and reports should all be on hand before you dial the number.
4. Be friendly, but get right to the point. This will save time for you and for the person you're calling.
5. Take time to recap your conversation and make sure you and the person you're calling agree on what you've covered and on what each of you will do as a follow-up. It can save you having to make another call later.
6. Listen carefully to everything the person says. Most conversations can be greatly shortened if you will follow the suggestions in the chapter on responsive listening.
7. Speak directly, distinctly, and clearly so you can avoid having to repeat things, or worse, having to deal with misunderstandings.
8. When you finish, hang up!

It might be helpful for you to pause and consider how you can apply these planning tips we've listed to other areas where people you work with are hampered by disturbances, distractions, and interruptions. Any investment you make in eliminating time wasters will help people (including yourself) to move toward high achievement.

Excess Baggage Item 3: Emotional Fatigue

One of the most common and unnecessary loads people have to carry is emotional fatigue. Medical experts say that more mistakes are made, production is slowed, and energy levels are reduced much more quickly when employees are upset, worried, or angry.

Of course, you cannot deal with all the personal problems people bring to your group activities. However, any effort you can make at eliminating factors that cause emotional fatigue in the workplace will be well invested.

For example, periodic breaks are valuable. Most major studies done during the last fifty years point out that breaks reduce fatigue, mistakes, and tension. Yet many business leaders either provide no breaks or give them grudgingly. Certainly breaks should be controlled by clear-cut guidelines, but periodic breaks geared to the times when people need them most can do wonders to help eliminate excess emotional fatigue.

Steps taken to assure people
their jobs are secure are usually
worth much more than they require
in time and effort.

Another hazard of the high-tech workplace is that people often fear for their security. When a major piece of equipment is being installed, rumors are apt to run rampant that as the equipment comes in, dozens of workers will go out. It seldom happens that way. In fact, studies show that most new installations either create more jobs or hold the level of employment steady. It is important that employees know that their jobs are secure. Keeping people guessing can create havoc with their emotions and actually can cause employees to try to sabotage the effectiveness of the new system. Steps taken to assure people their jobs are secure are usually worth much more than they require in time and effort.

Responsive leaders know that people are not like machines; people have emotional needs that, when met, can reduce the excess baggage of emotional fatigue and enable them to perform at peak levels. The following list serves as a reminder of emotional needs we all have—they all begin with the letter *A:*

- *Affection.* People need the warmth of good human relations.
- *Attention.* People need responsiveness to their requests or questions, even when the answer is no.
- *Appreciation.* People need approval; sincere compliments cost nothing and pay big dividends.
- *Accomplishment.* People need the sense of feeling worthwhile and the confidence that come from achievement.
- *Acceptance.* People need to know they are accepted, warts and all.
- *Affiliation.* People are social creatures; they thrive on identification with worthwhile teams.
- *Assurance.* People need the security of knowing they'll have a job tomorrow.
- *Accountability.* High-performance people enjoy performance reviews and appreciate the opportunity to report regularly that they are doing their jobs well.

If you want to enable people to work at peak levels, do everything you can to eliminate emotional fatigue.

TYING IT ALL TOGETHER

Family, friends, and coworkers benefit when you are attentive to their needs as they seek high achievement. By anticipating the desired equipment and environment, responsive leaders allow potential high achievers to concentrate their energies on their goals.

Responsive leaders know that people can perform at their peak only when they are free to climb fully equipped. Thus they provide expert guidance, all the resources people need to be effective, and as much freedom from excess baggage as possible.

TWELVE

How to Hold Responsive Meetings

Meetings can be either great time wasters or very useful gatherings—it all depends on how well leaders plan and how responsive they are.

Responsive leaders know that meetings hold tremendous potential because they bring together a wide range of people—with varying skills, resources, and ideas—who can accomplish a lot in a very short time. Thus, responsive leaders work hard to develop their skills for conducting productive meetings.

What makes a meeting productive? More than anything else, a productive meeting depends on its planning and execution. Meetings should be planned to draw maximum response from all who attend. This chapter discusses (1) questions to ask in planning for responsive, productive meetings; (2) guidelines for problem-solving meetings; (3) tips for opportunity exploration; and (4) suggestions for meetings that inform and motivate.

QUESTIONS FOR RESPONSIVE, PRODUCTIVE MEETINGS

"Let's get our heads together and see if we can come up with something." Thus begin some of the most disastrous and unproductive meetings ever held. But it doesn't have to be that way. Here are a dozen questions that can enable you to plan meetings that are both productive and responsive:

Question 1: Is This Meeting Really Needed?

Sometimes the most productive thing you can do is to refuse to hold—or to call off—a meeting. Busy people resist meetings that have no clear-cut justification. A good rule to follow is this: If you can get done what needs to be done without a meeting, then don't hold one.

It is always a good idea to ask, "Why is this meeting necessary?" and "What would happen if we didn't meet now?"

Question 2: What Is the Reason for Holding This Meeting?

There are basically three good reasons to hold a meeting: (1) You want to solve a problem; (2) you want to take advantage of an opportunity; and (3) you want to inform and/or motivate people.

A well-planned meeting can do some of all of those three things, but it is usually helpful to let one of them dominate.

Question 3: What Is the Goal of This Meeting?

What would you like for the meeting to accomplish? One good way to answer that is to ask yourself another question, "If this meeting had already been held, what positive impact would I have liked it to produce?" The more specifically you can answer those questions, the better your chances of having a good productive meeting.

Question 4: Who Should Attend This Meeting?

As a rule, only those people who have a clear reason for being there should attend. Responsive leaders always seek to call together only those people who are needed to get the job done.

Question 5: Who Should Lead the Meeting?

Sometimes, the most productive thing a leader can do is to ask someone else to conduct a meeting. People who lead meetings simply because they are "the boss" or because they have been drafted for the job can seldom be as productive as those who lead for some specific reason.

Question 6: What Procedures and Rules Will Guide the Meeting?

Just getting together and talking about something can result in a meeting that lasts all day and accomplishes nothing. It is crucial that you have a clear-cut procedure in mind, that all persons present understand that procedure, and that the procedure is followed precisely.

Question 7: Where Should the Meeting Be Held?

The first consideration is to find a productive location—private, comfortable (but not too comfortable), and

---

The better prepared people are to act,
the more productive they can be
when they get together.

---

equipped with resources needed to conduct business. A second consideration is to choose a location that will cost the most attendees the least in travel time both to and from the meeting.

Question 8: How Will Participants Be Informed Before the Meeting?

What information should be sent to participants before the meeting, and who will send it? The better prepared people are to act, the more productive they can be when they get together. Budgets, detailed reports, routine proposals, minutes, and instructions should all be digested by people before they come to the meeting. Having a group sit around and read together is almost always a time waster. Clear-cut instructions should be given to assure that the designated person sends the information to participants early enough, and that participants know they are expected to understand its contents before they come to the meeting.

Question 9: How Will Participants Be Informed During the Meeting?

What information should be given out at the meeting, how will it be given, and who will prepare and present it? Potentially explosive issues, radical new ideas, and major announcements are often best handled by a formal presentation at the meeting. Concise handouts, clear and attractive audiovisuals, and carefully constructed work sheets often can be effective for presenting complex issues and leading participants toward consensus. However, just giving people a stack of paper so "they'll feel like they've been to a meeting" is seldom productive. Most of the paper will end up in the trash can. Make it clear who will put together all the materials, how the materials will be prepared, and who will present them.

Question 10: When Should the Meeting Begin?

Careful consideration should be given to scheduling meetings at the most convenient time for the most participants. Perhaps an even greater priority is that the meeting should begin on time. Leaders face a challenge to get people to show up, ready to do business, before the scheduled time, and yet this skill is one of the most crucial factors in assuring the success of your meeting. Make it clear to all concerned that you will start on time, that key issues will be discussed early, and that coming in late is inconsiderate. Handle late arrivals by leaving empty seats near the door to minimize disturbances. If you stick to those principles, people will develop the habit of showing up on time.

Question 11: When Should the Meeting End?

It is almost always a good idea to have a definite time for the meeting to end and then to stick to it. People become frustrated when a meeting drags on and on, or when it ends abruptly because too much time was wasted discussing minor issues. Participants usually appreciate it when a leader keeps things moving at a deliberate but productive pace, makes sure all major issues get adequate attention, and assures that all items on the agenda have been handled before the scheduled ending time. They'll love you if you get good enough at it to let them out consistently early.

A meeting is only worth having when
it produces the result you desire.

Question 12: What Should Be Done to Follow Up the Meeting?

A meeting is only worth having when it produces the result you desire. The best way to assure that your goals are accomplished is to plan in advance who will follow up each decision, how they will follow it up, and how their follow-up will be reported to members of the group. Of course, you can't always predict how issues will be handled, or what new ideas will come up, but it always helps to have a standardized follow-up procedure.

More than anything else, productive meetings are the result of careful and adequate planning by responsive leaders. Even in those rare instances when an emergency meeting must be held, wise leaders invest the time spent waiting for people to assemble to get a clear handle on what should be accomplished and how to make sure it is achieved.

If an issue is important enough to justify holding a meeting, it is important enough to ask the above twelve questions. If it's not that important, don't hold the meeting.

All productive meetings are responsive meetings—whether their purpose is to solve problems, to take advantage of opportunities, or to inform and motivate. Responsive leaders always expect something positive to happen as a result of a meeting, even if what happens is that the group decides to do nothing about the issues raised.

GUIDELINES FOR PROBLEM-SOLVING MEETINGS

Productive meetings don't just happen. Productive meetings are led by responsive leaders who know how to get results. Here are some guidelines I have found useful in leading problem-solving meetings in my business, in my civic work, in my church, and even with my family.

Guideline 1: Define the Problem

Don't jump over this one, yet! I know it sounds obvious, but we often waste time by trying to solve problems we (and others) don't understand. In fact, the more people in a meeting, the less likely it is that all of them will understand the real problem. I find it very helpful to

1. Allow the person who perceives the problem to state it as clearly and succinctly as possible.
2. Lead the group in a brief discussion about the nature of the problem. Ask questions about such things as who is affected by the problem and how, how it affects the goals of the group, and what might happen if it's not solved. Avoid the temptation to explore possible solutions at this point. Concentrate entirely on bringing the problem clearly into focus.
3. Lead the group to a consensus as to what the problem really is. You might have to mediate some disputes, but creative tension can be helpful in solving problems.

Guideline 2: Consider All Reasonable Solutions

Virtually all problems have more than one solution—at least in the minds of diverse people. By allowing people to

---

> Virtually all problems have
> more than one solution.

---

express their views, you'll not only avoid later conflicts, but you'll often pick up valuable ideas. Steps include the following:

1. List ideas for solving the problem. It helps to write them on a flip chart or chalkboard, in the order in which they come up. Complete the list before allowing anyone to choose one or evaluate any of them.
2. Lead the group in a brief discussion of the relative merits of each proposal. Zero in on the few that seem to offer the most promise.
3. Project most likely outcomes of all viable alternatives.

Guideline 3: Decide and Act

As your group explores the various alternatives, one or two will begin to emerge as the most feasible. As soon as you sense that the group is near consensus, begin moving toward a decision.

1. Choose a course of action, either by vote or consensus. If you don't feel the group has enough information to make a decision, make assignments for gathering the data you need and then adjourn the meeting. It's a waste of time to sit around talking about a problem if you lack sufficient information to resolve it.
2. Make assignments for specific actions. Make sure each person present knows what he or she is expected to do in response to the decision the group has reached. Ask for feedback to make sure everyone understands.
3. List follow-up procedures. If necessary, set a date and time for a follow-up meeting, and list all the things that should be done before that meeting. If no follow-up

meeting is required, establish reporting procedures to assure fulfillment.

Guideline 4: Adjourn or Move on to the Next Item of Business

If you've done a thorough job of following the first three guidelines, this one should be self-evident. Yet most of us have little difficulty remembering meetings in which people were allowed to return again and again to issues that had already been settled. If the majority has agreed with the decision, get on with doing it.

TIPS FOR OPPORTUNITY EXPLORATIONS

The guidelines for exploring opportunities are identical to those for solving problems. All you need to do is to substitute the word *opportunity* for the word *problem* in each of the guidelines.

As a matter of fact, most opportunities first appear as problems. Of course, the terms are a little different. You'll be talking about options instead of solutions, but the principles are the same.

Here are some tips to help you take better advantage of the many opportunities that come your way.

Tip 1: Be Open to New Ideas

Always be open to new ideas—no matter who presents them. Some of the best ideas come from some of the least likely people. Even if you don't take someone's suggestion, it's great human relations to create a climate in which people feel they can be heard.

Tip 2: Stick to Your Goals

Always stick to your goals and stay consistent with your purpose. Every new opportunity prompts the question, "How will it affect our goals?" Many great opportunities will have to be rejected because they don't mesh with your goals. Any opportunity that forces you to restructure your goals or leads you away from your goals (even temporarily) should result in a complete rethinking of that opportunity and how it relates to your purpose.

Tip 3: Weigh All New Opportunities

Always weigh new opportunities against the impact they will have on other opportunities. Chasing new opportunities might be great fun, but it is usually more productive to make your existing commitments work. If a new option bleeds off resources you need for important projects you're now doing, pass it up, no matter how great it seems.

Tip 4: Take People Seriously

Always take seriously the people who present opportunities to you—even when you must reject their proposals. Two of the most common creativity stiflers are (1) making the person who brought up the idea feel dumb and (2) grabbing somebody's idea and running with it, without giving proper credit for it.

> If it's worth calling busy people
> together to hear,
> it's worth your best efforts
> to get it across.

If you must reject an idea, do so graciously with an honest explanation of why you turned it down. In any event, express gratitude to them for bringing it to your attention and smile.

Tip 5: Never Commit Others

Never commit others to opportunities without their knowledge and consent. With a little creativity and effort, you can gain commitment from most people you work with—even when the opportunity means extra work or difficulty for them. But it's a whole lot easier to gain that commitment in advance rather than after the fact.

SUGGESTIONS FOR MEETINGS THAT INFORM AND MOTIVATE

Meetings you hold to inform and motivate people are totally different ball games from those in which you seek to solve problems or consider opportunities.

When you say you're going to inform and motivate people, you imply that you have already reached a decision about what to do and that you're seeking to gain cooperation.

Yet, despite that major difference, your goal is precisely the same—you want to get people to understand and to act. The most effective way to do this is to involve them as much as possible in the process.

The best working definition of *inform* is "to make one aware of something." That means you have not informed someone until that person has become aware. It's another way of saying that you have taught only when someone has understood.

Likewise, the word *motivate* suggests "to cause to act."

You may give a rousing speech, but if people yawn and say, "So what," you haven't motivated them.

Audience response, therefore, is always the underlying goal of every informational and motivational meeting.

But how do you gain the response you desire? The points we discussed in the chapters on listening and communicating apply here. Yet there are some special considerations for a meeting where you seek to inform and motivate others. In many ways, it's the greatest test of your leadership. Here are some suggestions that can help make you more effective at it:

Suggestion 1: Be Clear and Concise

Define clearly and concisely what you want to get across. Boil it down to the bare essentials. It's best if you try to cover only one major point (three maximum) per session and support it with the least amount of data needed.

Suggestion 2: Know Your Audience

Learn as much as you can about the people who will attend the meeting. What do they know? What do they not know? What do they feel? What do they want? What makes them sit up and take notice? Remember, to get your audience to respond to you, you must be responsive to them.

Suggestion 3: Organize Your Information

Organize your material around your most compelling argument or information. Look for the note that strikes a responsive chord, and play it like a recurring theme in a beautiful concerto.

Suggestion 4: Prepare Carefully

Choose carefully how you will present it. Studies show that people (on average) retain about 10 percent of what they hear, about 20 percent of what they hear and see, and about 50 percent of what they practice doing—and that after only 24 hours.

Suggestion 5: Involve Your Listeners

Choose carefully how you will involve them in the learning process. One of the best techniques is to lead people through questions to discover what you want them to know.

Suggestion 6: Do Your Best

Give it your best shot. If it's worth calling busy people together to hear, it's worth your best efforts to get it across.

Suggestion 7: Test Your Response

Test constantly—not your audience, but yourself. Keep checking until you are sure they have understood what you wanted to say. After the meeting, follow up carefully to see that they are doing what you asked them to do.

TYING IT ALL TOGETHER

As a rule, the more responsive your meetings are, the greater response you can expect from those who attend. Meetings that are carefully planned, conducted by effective guidelines, and followed up carefully can be powerful tools for accomplishing your goals.

This is true whether you are involved with family members planning a holiday party, friends planning a weekend trip to the mountains, or colleagues planning a new ad campaign. Vague goals and ambiguous decisions will undermine the effectiveness of your meetings; clear goals and clear decisions will enhance your possibilities for success.

THIRTEEN

How to Be a Tiger, Not a Pussycat

In the Preface, I told you that responsive people are tigers, not pussycats. They meet the world head-on and give freely of themselves to learn how to relate to and work successfully with other people. They are responsive to the needs, desires, and concerns of others, and because they are, they develop people power. Their positive approach to human relationships helps them reap benefits not shared by unresponsive people.

The smallest package in the world is a person all wrapped up in himself. If you don't believe that's true, just look at what happens to people who are totally unresponsive to others.

Some of the most unresponsive people in the world can be found in our nation's prisons. They got there by thinking only of themselves—what *they* wanted, what *they* needed, what *they* were concerned with. That's why we call them "hardened criminals." They've *hardened themselves* to the people around them. They didn't choose responsiveness.

Other unresponsive people end up in mental hospitals because they'd rather withdraw from reality than risk reaching out to others. Some even commit suicide because they can't stand the pain of being alone. They didn't choose responsiveness.

Unresponsive people always seem to end up "victims." They have a way of needing others to care for them, to make their decisions for them, and often even to lock them up so they won't hurt themselves or others.

> The smallest package in the world is
> a person all wrapped up in himself.

This chapter discusses (1) your greatest emotional need; (2) the traits of responsive people; and (3) pointers for becoming a more responsive person.

YOUR GREATEST EMOTIONAL NEED

Your greatest emotional need—the need to love and be loved—can be met only by God and by other people.

One of the most dramatic stories I ever heard concerned a maternity clinic in a major city, where babies of unwed indigent mothers were kept until they were old enough to be adopted. The babies were dying at a rate several times greater than that of other maternity wards, and nobody could figure out why. Clinic personnel enforced sterile techniques against the possibility that diseases and infections might be creeping in. They tried different formulas to feed the infants, and they looked for answers in the prenatal care of the mothers.

Finally, an elderly cleaning woman called a doctor aside and announced, "I know why the babies are dying!"

"Please tell me," he pleaded. "We've tried everything, and we haven't been able to stop them from dying."

"Well . . . ," she drawled, "it isn't natural for babies not to be loved. These babies have never seen their mamas, nobody ever holds them, or talks to them, or sings to them. They're starving for love."

Volunteers were recruited to come in for several hours each day just to hold, rock, and talk or sing to the babies. Almost overnight, the mortality rate dropped to normal.

Human beings were created to be responsive creatures. It's as natural for us to respond to others, and to seek response from others, as it is for us to breathe and eat.

In fact, responsiveness is so natural that we have to cultivate the habit of withdrawing from people. And, unfortunately, unresponsiveness is a most destructive habit.

But unresponsiveness, like all habits, can be broken by practicing the new habit of responsiveness until it becomes automatic.

I'd like to leave you with some pointers I've discovered about developing a responsive lifestyle, but first let's look more closely at the kind of person you will become if you practice responsiveness.

TRAITS OF THE MOST BEAUTIFUL PEOPLE IN THE WORLD

The most beautiful people in the world are those who are most responsive to others; and the more responsive they are, the more beautiful they become.

Here are some of the traits by which you can readily recognize responsive people:

Trait 1: Responsive People Are Assertive

That may surprise you, but think about it. It's not that they always stand up for their rights; it's more that they value themselves and others enough not to let themselves be walked on. They know they have a lot to give, and they persist in giving it. They get respect by earning it, not by demanding it.

Trait 2: Responsive People Are Forceful

Far from being like Milquetoast, responsive people are compelling. They have a way of getting things done by making people want to do them. They seek to influence rather than to coerce.

Trait 3: Responsive People Are Persuasive

You'll find responsive people making their appeal to the self-interest of others, and that's the most persuasive approach of all. By giving what they want, they persuade others to respond in like fashion.

Trait 4: Responsive People Are Approachable

Secure in their knowledge of who they are, responsive people are not defensive. People find them easy to approach and always willing to listen to their concerns.

Trait 5: Responsive People Are Gracious

Responsive people treat all people with dignity, and they concern themselves with how others feel and think. Even when they must disagree with, or say no to, someone, they do it with warmth, kindness, and a smile.

Trait 6: Responsive People Are Patient

Since it's taken a long time for them to develop, responsive people understand that others must be given time, too. So they keep on being responsive—no matter what.

Trait 7: Responsive People Are Humble

Responsive people know they have a place in the universe, but not at its center. They're grateful for what they have received, and they gladly share all they have and are with others.

Trait 8: Responsive People Are Productive

You'll find responsive people cooperating freely with all people because they know it's the best way to gain cooperation. Long ago, they learned that one of the master keys to productivity is having a lot of people help you along the way.

Trait 9: Responsive People Are Successful

Responsive people define success as having a purpose for life and as fulfilling that purpose through their goals. Since their purpose and goals are built around giving themselves to others, they are successful from the first day they commit themselves to give it their best shot.

Trait 10: Responsive People Are Effective

Knowing that their productivity depends on getting a lot of people to help them, responsive people get out of themselves and give freely to others. Thus they always have plenty of people who are willing to help them get the job done.

In short, responsive people

1. Value people (including themselves) above everything but God.

2. Give to people what they want most to get.

3. Make cooperation a way of life.

4. Keep doing it . . . throughout their whole lives.

POINTERS FOR BECOMING
A MORE RESPONSIVE PERSON

Living responsively is the best way to live in this high-tech world; it's the only way to relate successfully to other people. And chances are pretty good you'd like to be more responsive, because you know it's the only way you can become the dynamic person you were created to be.

One theme has echoed through this entire book. You'll get more of what you're looking for if you make responsiveness a way of life. In this unresponsive high-tech world, being responsive to others is like being a spring of fresh, clear water in a desert—people will come to you and drink freely of what you have to offer.

You'll get more of what you're looking for
if you make responsiveness a way of life.

All of us can become more responsive every day of our lives. Here are some pointers I've found useful in my search to become the responsive person God created me to be. I hope you will use them to become one of the most beautiful people in the world.

Pointer 1: Master the High Art
of Giving Yourself Away

More and more people are waking up to the myth of self-motivation—the idea that we are totally self-contained beings and that the way to be happy is to build our world around ourselves. Self-motivation is built on self-deception.

Some exciting things began to happen in my life when I got away from self–motivation and started living by out-of-self–motivation. When I began to make God the center of my life, and other people the focal point of my goals and activities, I found myself achieving more and enjoying it at a deeper level. Much to my surprise, I've lived more abundantly than I ever dreamed I could, accomplished more with my time, and gained more cooperation from people. (I tell more about how to do this in my first book, *Peak Performance Principles for High Achievers*.)

Giving yourself away means adopting the golden rule as a lifestyle. It means more than simply not treating people the way you would not want to be treated. That's only the negative side. The positive side is that you consciously search for ways to give people what you want most to get. Gradually, you become aware that the joy of life comes from giving yourself away, and what you get in return is only a bonus.

Pointer 2: Become a Risk-Taker

Unresponsive people are afraid they'll get hurt if they reach out to others, so they hold back. Responsive people know that others will sometimes hurt them, but they're willing to take the risk anyway. Why?

1. Responsive people know that nothing could be worse than becoming numb to others. The really pitiful people in our world are those who have shut themselves off from others and who feel neither pain nor joy. They're walking around like zombies. Responsive people would

> Responsive people would not choose
> to be hurt by others,
> but even that is better than
> the emptiness of feeling nothing.

not choose to be hurt by others, but even that is better
than the emptiness of feeling nothing.
2. Responsive people know that pain is seldom the awesome monster they've been led to believe. Pain is never
fatal, and it can be very useful. It can cause us to pay
attention to the underlying cause that produces it, it can
lead us to increase our resolve to rise above it, and it can
cause us to seek the only real cure for it—reaching out to
others.
3. Responsive people know that the pain that comes from
conflict is the price we pay for growing intimacy with
others.
4. Responsive people know that trying to reduce the risk of
pain by not reaching out keeps them from enjoying the
tremendous fulfillment of human relationships.

In a very real sense, reaching out to others is the least
risky route of all.

Pointer 3: Practice Awareness

Everything in our high-tech world deadens our sensitivity. Pills and propaganda mask our headaches. Shock ab-
sorbers shield us from the bumps of the road. Loud music
blots out the unwanted thoughts of our minds.

Awareness suggests such attitudes as being alert, awake to the realities of life, vigilant, on-guard lest we miss something important, and sensitive to the beauty around us.

We have to practice being aware. For example, it's easy to find ourselves so frustrated by traffic jams and discourteous drivers that we never see the gorgeous sunset that is ours for the taking.

Practicing awareness of people involves observing what they do, listening to what they say, and receiving the exciting realities they bring to us.

Responsive people know that awareness comes only from a constant effort to overcome the deadening influences of worry, preoccupation, and anxiety.

Pointer 4: Conquer Stress and Tension

Nothing blocks out your responsiveness like being uptight. Tension can make you miss valuable opportunities to reach out, make you irritable and insensitive to the needs and feelings of others, and rob you of the joys of working with others for high achievement.

If you've chosen to be a high achiever, you will always be faced with pressing deadlines and schedules, demanding tasks, and obstacles that must be overcome.

The best way to triumph over tension is to consciously practice positive doing, "Okay! Where do we go from here?"

Pointer 5: Build a Responsive Vocabulary

Obviously a responsive vocabulary includes words like *please* and *thank you*. But it contains much more than that.

For example, "Why would he or she do that?" is a responsive phrase because it seeks to understand the motivations of others. "That's a great idea!" is another one. Or what about, "I know it hurts, and I care." Or, "Wow! You're really something special."

You get the idea, don't you? You build a vocabulary that shows how much you value people, how much you want to understand their needs, and how seriously you take what matters to them. The more you practice, the better you'll get.

Pointer 6: Practice Making Others Feel Important

Do you know people who are always glad to see you? *Really* glad? So glad that their faces light up when you come around? Doesn't it make you feel special?

Mary Kay Ash, the cosmetics tycoon mentioned earlier, says that every person you meet wears an invisible sign that says, MAKE ME FEEL IMPORTANT. People become responsive to you when you make them feel important.

But the real fun of it comes from making people who are considered nobodies feel like somebodies. Anybody can be nice to millionaires who might give them some money, or to influential people who might speak a word in their behalf. But the real joy of responsive living comes from treating ordinary people as if they are really special.

> There are no ordinary people,
> only important people
> who don't know it yet.

Responsive people soon learn that there are no ordinary people, only important people who don't know it yet.

Pointer 7: Keep Your Priorities Straight

The responsive leader *values* people and *uses* things. That sounds so simple as to be almost trite, but in practice, it is incredibly easy to reverse the two.

For example, ask almost any business leader what's the most important thing in his or her life, and you'll often get the response, "My family." Yet, if you ask that person where he or she invests the most time and creative energies, the answer will likely be, "Work."

If people matter most to you, constantly and consciously make them your highest priority.

Pointer 8: Be a Host, Not a Guest

Some people always act as if they are guests in this world and everybody else is here to serve them. You'll see them throwing litter out on highways, barging in front of others in a line, and talking so loud in public places that nobody else can carry on a conversation.

But responsive people are more like hosts. They don't move out and let others take over their homes or offices, but they do try to make others feel welcome. They are considerate, and they treat all people with dignity.

> The secret is to make
> yourself teachable.

Hosts are nice people to be around. They treat life as a banquet table and their family members, friends, and fellow workers are their guests.

Pointer 9: Always Remain Teachable

One of the greatest benefits of being responsive is that you're always learning so many exciting things. And fantastic teachers are everywhere you look. Remember the cleaning woman who taught a medical doctor something far more valuable than what he'd learned in medical school?

Teachers are everywhere. The secret is to make yourself teachable—to be humble enough, curious enough, and interested enough to unlock the hidden treasures of those around you.

Pointer 10: Cultivate Intimacy

Isn't it exciting what often happens to a hard-nosed executive who suddenly becomes a grandfather? More and more frequently his secretary will say, "He's out of the office." He's out with that grandchild! He's pushing swings and fishing and taking long walks.

Then you begin to notice some other things. He smiles more freely, becomes more understanding of employees whose children are sick, and even starts pausing to look at the pictures of children on his secretary's desk.

That's the kind of stuff intimacy does to you. It makes you tear down that ivory tower facade you've been living behind. It makes you aware of colors and hues you haven't noticed in years, and it can even make you whistle a happy tune.

Sharing intimate moments with those you love makes you more responsive to people you work with and those you meet along the way. The more intimacy you share, the more responsive you become.

TYING IT ALL TOGETHER—AND LOOKING AHEAD

As we look to the future through the theme of this book, two things appear certain:

1. The more our world becomes addicted to high-tech gadgets, the less responsive it will become. Machines simply do not have the capacity to love or to value people.
2. Those people who remain responsive to others will always be in great demand. It's a simple matter of the law of supply and demand. The colder and less sensitive the environment, the greater the need for responsive people in all areas of life.

I can safely promise you that if you'll make the Dynamic Responsiveness System a way of life, you'll become a powerful and exciting person.

Much more could have been said about the subject. I could have given you some detailed rules designed to help you deal with specific situations. But that's not what responsiveness is all about.

Dynamic Responsiveness is an attitude, a lifestyle, a way of thinking about and acting toward people. The one element that remains constant in our ever-changing world is our freedom to choose how we will respond to others. Thus, no matter how confusing things get, we can choose in advance how we will respond to people. As we do, we can not only adjust to rapid changes, but we can also shape (rather than be shaped by) our environment.

The practical outworking of the basic ideas of this book I leave to you. Instead of suggesting that you "do as I say or as I have done," I urge you to use these ideas to forge a down-to-earth system you can live with and use to good advantage. Let it work in your own life and in all your relationships.

I hope I've given you enough guidelines and inspiration to encourage you to try it for yourself. Believe me, I am a fellow struggler, but I think it's the only way to live! Responsively!

INFORMATION

For information on John Noe's speaking engagements, consulting services, video and audio tapes, or industrial housekeeping management systems and training, please contact:

Industrial Housekeeping Management Systems, Inc.
6848 Hawthorn Park Drive
Indianapolis, IN 46220
(317) 841-7777

Other Books by the Author

Peak Performance Principles for High Achievers is John Noe's dramatic true story of how he transformed himself, sedentary and out-of-shape in his mid-thirties, into the dynamic leader he is today—and how you can too.